Guerrilla Marketing Excellence
Goes for the Gold!

"In the marketing world, no one knows how to use the weapons of the trade better than industry expert Jay Levinson. He is living proof that his unconventional marketing ideas work."

—*Entrepreneur*

"Once again, in *Guerrilla Marketing Excellence*, Jay Conrad Levinson offers us a banquet of common sense. This book is a guide through today's economic minefield with marketing principles of action and pearls of experience."

—James R. Bryant, President
Renaissance Vineyard & Winery

"Every page has enough marketing tips to inspire whole campaigns. Indeed, if more marketing professionals followed at least some of Levinson's rules, their campaigns would be more successful and their customers better served. Anyone, in any field or profession, who values innovation and excellence will benefit from *Guerrilla Marketing Excellence*."

—*Dow Jones News*

"Jay Levinson is my choice for remodelers. Levinson's books target small businesses and have literally hundreds of ready-to-use ideas. Guerrilla Marketing books are a great start in getting educated."

—Linda W. Case, President
Remodeling Consulting Services

"Fifty ways to leave your marketing miseries behind, this is Jay Levinson's best book ever—original wit and wisdom from the practical prophet of money making marketing. Absolutely the best!"

—John Caple, author of *On Purpose*
and *The Ultimate Interview*

EATING LIFE
Guerrilla Marketing's Golden Rule #50:

*If you don't take control of your marketing,
your company's future will be in the
hands of your competitors.*

GUERRILLA MARKETING EXCELLENCE

The 50 Golden Rules
for Small-Business Success

by the author of *Guerrilla Marketing*

JAY CONRAD LEVINSON

HOUGHTON MIFFLIN COMPANY

Boston   New York

For information about permission to reproduce selections
from this book, write to Permissions, Houghton Mifflin Company,
215 Park Avenue South, New York, New York 10003.

Library of Congress Cataloging-in-Publication Data

Levinson, Jay Conrad.
Guerrilla marketing excellence: The 50 Golden Rules for Small-Business
Success / Jay Conrad Levinson.
p.   cm.
ISBN 0-395-60844-9 (pbk.)
1. Marketing.   2. Small business—Management.   3. Advertising.
I. Title.
HF5415.L4793   1993
658.8—dc20   92-20533   CIP

Printed in the United States of America
MP   10   9   8   7   6   5   4   3

This book is dedicated
to the remarkable people
who have provided me with
the invaluable energy of their
encouragement, expertise, and strokes:

Michael Larsen
Elizabeth Pomada
Bill Shear
Leo Burnett
Howard Gossage
Mike Lavin
John Caple
Elaine Petrocelli
Bobby Diamond

and my ever-loving guerrilla wife,
Pat Levinson

Contents

Preface

How Guerrillas Profit from Golden Rules

THE PAST THREE Guerrilla Marketing books were devoted to how-to-do-it-marketing. This book will show you how to do it with excellence.

This is the book that will steer you clear of painful pitfalls while setting you on a course toward increased profits. It will help you avoid contributing to the enormous sum of money that is wasted each year on misguided marketing by well-meaning business owners.

While it is true that the guerrilla knows that marketing is like a game that can be fun to play, that same guerrilla knows that the game is played for real money. So it's no place for kids, amateurs, or phonies. How you think about marketing has a dramatic effect upon how well it works for you. This book is written so that you will think about it in ways that will enhance your bottom line.

Playing for real money

The topics covered in *Guerrilla Marketing Excellence* aren't part of standard textbook marketing, yet they're far too important to overlook if you're interested in making significant contributions to the profitability of your business. The guidelines for guerrillas in my previous books were target-directed. The guidelines in the upcoming pages fine-tune that aim to the center of the bull's-eye.

The advice in these pages appears in the guise of basic home truths, many of which are already part of your own good common sense. But common sense, as I learn daily, isn't all that common. As a guerrilla, it is crucial that you know all these truths. But that's not enough. Additionally, you must possess the guerrilla's attitude. That attitude is characterized by the word *knowledge*. If you have the right knowledge, you won't be tempted to become a rule-breaker, even when your patience is wearing thin. Obviously, it is not a good idea to break a golden rule.

Knowledge of these rules will be reflected in your profits. Practicing them will put teeth into all of your marketing by removing any naiveté or nonsensical notions. Knowledge will elevate your marketing expertise and understanding to the point where competitors hold you in awe, prospects will be powerfully attracted to your offerings, and customers will reciprocate the respect you feel for them in the form of repeat business and enthusiastic referrals.

Some large corporations get around these rules with bottomless bank accounts. But most small businesses haven't the luxury of ignorance and plentitude. They must learn what guerrillas know so each dollar can do the work of many.

Toppling your idols

If anything that appears in these pages goes against your grain or topples any of your idols, I don't apologize, for that's exactly my intention. It means you're getting the point. It means you're learning the rules.

Guerrillas, like Olympic athletes, go for the gold. These golden rules enable you to do the same. They set you up to succeed by indoctrinating you in the nuances of marketing, the small but omnipotent details untouched by most marketing courses, unpracticed by many marketing departments.

If I may be candid a moment, and let's see you try to stop me, most marketing in America is generally horrible. When you notice a company grow, gain positive word-of-mouth, prosper, and continue to succeed, it is very likely because that company is practicing guerrilla marketing's golden rules, consciously or not, and realizes that the rules lead to higher profits and more focused marketing.

The Gap clothing store chain started small, became large, and practiced these golden rules all along. Santa Rosa Bedding Company started with little more than a knowledge of these rules, yet took less than three years to become the dominant bedding store in one of California's fastest-growing cities, marketing with television and newspapers almost from Day One. Store owner Carolyn Lavin Dutrow doesn't look like a guerrilla but sure acts like one with her unswerving devotion to the guerrilla's golden rules.

As a guerrilla yourself, or a guerrilla in training, you should know that you've got to be guided by a simple guerrilla marketing strategy, piloted by a guerrilla marketing calendar, and armed with an arsenal brimming with guerrilla marketing weapons.

Those tools, plus knowledge of these rules, will enable you to take your fair share — or even much more — from the land of plenty. That's where your prospects hail from.

The land of plenty

Businesspeople who approach marketing without a framework take wild risks with their marketing even though they sincerely believe they are following a conservative course. What you don't know *will* hurt you in this arena, and often hurt your prospects and customers at the same time.

Is it important that you know every one of these golden rules? Absolutely. Is it necessary that you follow each rule in all your marketing forays? No way, José. But a true guerrilla thinker knows the rules he or she is intentionally breaking rather than breaking them unintentionally and leaving him or herself open to disaster.

Of course, the rules are constantly changing. But golden rules contain some basic truths that change much more slowly. And some never change at all. There's nothing to lose by knowing the rules. But there's much to lose by being oblivious to them.

The guerrilla business owner who knows these rules knows *how to think about marketing,* a talent many competitors never develop. Their actions in business are clinics in marketing expertise, reflecting their knowledge and perception of the guerrilla approach.

Guerrilla marketing's 50 golden rules are yours to follow or to ignore. Here, they are presented to you without the need for extensive searching or an MBA with a concentration in marketing. This is an entire bookful of rules that can make or break a company. It's that simple and that important.

Guerrilla marketing's 50 golden rules are yours to follow or to ignore. Your company and your future are dependent upon your decision.

Part One
Golden Rules to Guide Your Thinking

What the Stonecutter Knows

Guerrilla Marketing's Golden Rule #1:
Blessed with the guerrilla's vision, do not seek instant gratification, but find your rewards with farsightedness.

WATCH THE POWERFUL stonecutter as he raises the hammer and hits the huge stone again and again, again and again. On the fifth blow, the stone splits in two.

Does that mean it took five blows of the hammer to do the big job? Of course not. It took 500, maybe 5,000 blows. The final blow wasn't important by itself, but only as one of many blows that combined to achieve the stonecutter's goal. To an unsophisticated observer, it took five blows of a hammer to split a rock. But the stonecutter and you know the real truth.

The real truth about marketing is that it is very much like **The real truth** stonecutting. Your trade show booth may not do the job. Your direct-mail letter won't do it either. But your booth plus your letter plus your telemarketing plus your advertising presence plus your publicity plus your time and your patience finally combine to get the job done.

Which blow gets the credit for breaking the rock? Which marketing weapon gets the credit for breaking the profit records?

The stonecutter gets all the credit for what has been hewn from the rock. The marketing director gets all the credit for the profits generated through marketing. It takes a unique person to stay the course while blow after blow fails to hit home. It takes extraordinary talent to remain with the marketing program when instant results are not produced.

Yet many members of the time-conscious public wonder if instant gratification is fast enough for them. This is a characteristic of many people, the guerrilla not included.

Great stonecutters know that there is no rock they cannot split. They have more patience than any rock. Great marketing people know there is no challenge they cannot surmount. They have more patience than their competition. They set lofty goals, then exhibit exemplary behavior in the pursuit of the goals.

The behavior is demonstrated in both their restraint from making changes in the marketing program and their willingness to continue with the program as planned, despite the absence of quick financial strokes.

Not for the get-rich-quick crowd

To quote a wise businessman: "The best executive is the one who has sense enough to pick good men to do what he wants done, and self-restraint enough to keep from meddling with them while they do it."

The stonecutter picks a spot on the rock and hammers at it over and over. The marketing honcho picks a niche and aims for it. Eventually — the rock splits. Eventually, the niche is occupied and dominated, the marketing goals attained. It didn't take genius as much as it took steadfastness.

Your life will be filled with antacids and anxiety if you expect your marketing, brilliant or otherwise, to produce superb results instantly. But if you give your marketing program — and having a program is paramount — the time to penetrate and motivate, to persuade and create desire, you will discover that it always works and that age-old techniques are the secret of its success.

There's a very good likelihood that all along you knew everything I've written. But why is it that the overwhelming majority of marketing fails because most marketing gets changed before it has a chance to work?

That is the downside of our penchant for doing things fast and saving as much time as possible. As noble as those endeavors may be, they are not the cornerstones for the stonecutter or the marketing director. Marketing is different from most human activities.

Be cool

No stonecutter approaches the rock in a rush. No stonecutter expects results in a hurry. But all stonecutters are positive that they can do the job they set out to do if they concentrate upon the results down the road rather than the hard rock surface facing them.

Karate experts will tell you that you cannot split a board with one stroke of your bare hand by concentrating on the point on the board where the impact will take place. They will say, however, that you can split a board with one stroke of your hand by concentrating on the point *beneath the board* where your hand will be after the impact takes place.

United States small businesses are populated by people who gaze intently at the board. So short a gaze reveals little and results in painful hands — or wasted marketing investments.

Guerrillas do not even acknowledge the board. It is insignificant compared with the place beneath it where their hand is headed. This farsighted approach shows them the way to their goal. They see that the way is not so much a route as an attitude. This is the attitude of the stonecutter. This is the mindset of the guerrilla. Both have what appears to the innocent as an impossible task. Both know that there is no way they will fail.

What board?

A client of mine used the principle of stonecutting in a unique manner. He was opening a store that specialized in beds and needed an ad for the Yellow Pages. What to say? What to show? How to do it best? What would the stonecutter do?

The client struck his first blow at the stone by visiting a large public library. He struck his next 100 blows by examining the Yellow Pages section under *Beds* in 100 different directories. He kept careful notes, using his ballpoint as his hammer.

He noted the best words, the best phrases, the unique claims. He studied the larger ads even more carefully, reasoning that these were successful operations and were going about things in the right way. With his hammer, he was meticulous in his research.

Then he combined the best elements of the best ads for the best bedding stores in the nation and crafted an ad for his Berkeley Design Shop that has pulled in bed-buyers for over

20 years. Each person who walks into the showroom is another rock-hewn masterpiece, the result of many blows of the hammer.

Did it happen instantly? Not at all. But it happens consistently because he followed the golden rule known to stonecutters and guerrillas.

Precision

Guerrilla Marketing's Golden Rule #2:
The ability to accurately define your precise market or markets dramatically affects your profitability.

THERE IS HARDLY anything shocking about this golden rule. What is shocking is the extremely high number of small businesses in America that fail to define the exact market they will serve.

Of the many marketing errors committed by small business owners — and the selection is embarrassingly large — this is one of the most glaring and common.

Take a one-question test to see if you happen to be guilty of this guerrilla marketing crime:

A one-question test

Suppose you were quizzed right now as to what business you are in or what your company is known for. What would your answer be?

If you can't say it in your mind without thinking for a long time, or if your answer is long and involved, you are guilty as sin of failure to position yourself clearly. You are making marketing's biggest error.

Guerrillas know they must focus on key groups in order to properly define their market. Here's how you can gain that clarity of focus for yourself:

First, *make a list of your ten best customers or clients.* Ask and answer seven questions about them:

Know thy customer

1. What do they read? Expend the energy the guerrilla requires to find out the names of these publications:
   City newspapers
   Community newspapers
   Industry newspapers

Trade magazines
Consumer magazines
Newsletters
2. What shows do they attend?
   National conventions
   Local trade shows
   Community events
3. To what groups do they belong?
   Business and professional groups
   Community groups
4. What do they respond to?
   Phone calls
   Letters
   On-site visits
   Any other marketing tools
5. How did they first hear about you?
   Mass media marketing
   Mini media marketing
   Word of mouth
6. Why do they continue to buy from you?
   Service
   Quality
   Rapport
7. What are their problems?

When you know the answers to the seven questions, read what those customers read. Attend the shows they attend. Join the groups they've joined. Get onto their wavelength as much as you can. Define your market in your mind.

Then use your newfound insights to communicate with prospects just as you communicate with customers. Exactly what is a prospect? It's a potential customer.

Doing something extra Stress the same benefits. Treat them better than any competitors ever have by *doing something extra*. Where can you find the prospects in the bull's-eye of your target? Three answers: (1) Let them find you through your vast arsenal of marketing weaponry that reaches out to offer your prime benefits and a chance to begin a dialogue — by means of a toll-free number or a response device such as a coupon; (2) Actively seek prospects in the form of direct referrals from your customers; (3) Act on the crucial data the seven questions gave you about media, shows, and groups.

Your continuing task as a guerrilla is to convince prospects that you can solve the problems they have and then to actually solve these problems when potential customers become real customers. To gain the proper perspective, visualize this task as a circle. One-half of the circle is made up of prospects who need problems solved. Because you *can* solve them, they become customers. Because you *did* solve them, they refer new prospects. That's the other half of the circle. Operating only within half the circle is what 95 percent of business owners do. But you must utilize the entire circle to make the most from what you offer.

There are not many things as valuable to a guerrilla as names of prospects and built-in introductions via the names of people they know — and all for free.

Throughout this book of golden rules, I have recommended the idea of a customer questionnaire. When you send yours, be certain to include the seven questions. And be committed up-front to act upon the information you will obtain.

It isn't worth your time to obtain the information if you neglect to do anything about it. *Action is the purpose of the exercise.*

Action is the purpose

Studying the answers to the seven questions will help you define your market. They will help you get a clear picture of your business. They will show you why you are succeeding or not. They will help you avoid marketing's biggest error, a lack of precise focus.

Knowing this is merely a start on achieving a clear focus. Marketing changes. People change. Times change. Media change. Priorities change. The answers to your seven questions will change. Some high-powered company is going to get the new answers to the questions so that they can make the best offer in the business.

And who will that high-powered company be? It will be your company because you have kept abreast of the changes. Every three years, send a new customer questionnaire. Ask the seven questions. Ask 10 or 20 more if you'd like. Ask what you've asked before, and ask what you've never asked.

Don't limit the questionnaires to customers only. Ask your own employees how they feel about your product or service. Some of the most valuable information you'll collect will come from ordinarily untapped resources: receptionists, secretaries, mail clerks, assistants, and others not too far from the bottom of the totem pole.

Only by constantly maintaining precision with these methods will you be able to keep an accurate aim at your market and minimize waste of your marketing dollars and precious time.

Companies throughout the land are operating with outmoded customer information, or more likely, none at all. That's why they fail to define their market. This golden rule could be their salvation.

What People Really Buy

Guerrilla Marketing's Golden Rule #3:
Gear your marketing to people already in the market, and know what they really buy other than instant gratification.

THERE ARE A MYRIAD of benefits that people seek from any given service or product. All you've got to do is consistently put across any one of those benefits to the people who want them *right now* and you've virtually made the sale.

People do not buy because marketing is glitzy but because marketing strikes a chord in the mind of the prospect that makes that person want the advantages of what you are selling. Marketing does not work because it sells products or services but because it helps people realize the merits of *owning* the products or services.

Striking a chord

To increase your enlightenment of what makes marketing work, you must know first and forever what customers really buy.

- They buy *benefits* and not features. That's obvious.
- They buy *promises* you make. So make them with care.
- They buy the promises they want *personally* fulfilled.
- They buy your *credibility,* or don't buy if you lack it.
- They buy *solutions* to their problems.
- They buy *you,* your *employees,* your *service department.*
- They buy *wealth, success, security, love, acceptance.*
- They buy your *guarantee, reputation,* and *good name.*
- They buy *other people's opinions* of your business.
- They buy *expectations* based upon your marketing.
- They buy *believable* claims, not simply honest claims.
- They buy *hope* for their own and their company's future.

- They buy *brand names* over strange names.
- They buy the *consistency* they've seen you exhibit.
- They buy the *stature* of the media in which you market.
- They buy *value* — which is not the same as price.
- They buy *selection*, and often the best of your selection.
- They buy *freedom from risk*, granted by your warranty.
- They buy *acceptance by others* of your goods and services.
- They buy *certainty*; no one reserved flights at Kittyhawk.
- They buy *convenience* in buying, paying, and lots more.
- They buy *respect* for their own ideas and personality.
- They buy your *identity* as conveyed by your marketing.
- They buy *clarity*; if they don't understand they don't buy.
- They buy *style* — the kind that fits their own style.
- They buy *neatness* and assume that's how you do business.
- They buy *honesty*; one dishonest word means no sale.
- They buy *comfort*, offerings that fit their comfort zone.
- They buy *success*: your success which can lead to theirs.
- They buy *good taste* and they know it from bad taste.

Guerrilla companies tell the right people what they'll be buying — the benefits just listed — when dealing with the company, and *that's* why marketing works. Marketing works because prospects are *reassured into becoming customers*, offered exactly what they want or need, and turned on enough to the benefits they are seeking on both a conscious and an unconscious level.

Reassurance does it

Marketing works because savvy companies realize what customers *do not* buy: fancy adjectives, clever headlines, special effects in marketing, items not fitting their self-identity, marketing that screams, marketing that sounds as though it is exaggerating, low price (though 14 percent do), unproven items, or gorgeous graphics that get in the way of the primary benefits.

Customers also don't buy humor that obfuscates benefits, offerings heralded with unreadable type, offerings marketed with copy that has poor grammar or misspelled words, salespeople who don't listen, or things they don't fully understand. People do not buy technical advancements that have no clear benefits, insincerity in any form, overpromises (even when true), shoddy quality or service, or even a trace of amateurism in your marketing.

The kinds of marketing that work steer clear of these sale-stoppers. Marketing works only if you understand what *works* really means. When marketing works, it builds your sales and your profits. It shows you your most profitable offerings along with the ones that aren't so profitable. It encourages your customers to come in more often and spend more money. It diverts prospects and profits from your competitors. It reminds customers and potential customers of your prime benefits. You may be bored hearing them; customers and prospects don't bore as easily. Finally, it establishes and maintains your identity and your reputation. Marketing works for businesses that establish these goals.

Marketing does not work for companies that have unrealistic expectations about the powers of marketing. Be clear on this. Marketing cannot create an instant influx of new customers, cause an immediate and dramatic increase in your profits, substitute for second-rate quality or service, solve all your cash flow problems, create a desire for unwanted products or services, or sell the right product to the wrong people, in the wrong place, or at the wrong time.

What marketing cannot do

What kind of marketing reaches the people who really buy? That's easy — marketing that *involves prospects and informs customers*. It can't do this unless it interests prospects and customers. It has an easier time doing this if it illustrates your benefits. Marketing works because it invites prospects to make a purchase. And marketing works because you know and practice the thing that makes it work — commitment to your marketing plan.

Fortunately for guerrillas, it is relatively simple to reach the people who buy and convince them that you have what they want. This is because there is so little great marketing being practiced, so little actually *getting through to people*. That's why, with the attitude and energy of a guerrilla, it is not difficult to stand apart from your competitors and to shine in the minds of your prospects.

People do need and want things, and marketing shows that these things are available, affordable, and desirable. It works because many people are about to make a purchase and honestly appreciate being steered in the right direction.

My first business suit

I recall when, fresh from college, I decided that I had to own a business suit. But where should I get it? How much should I pay for it? And what should I look for in a suit? Coincidentally, though it rarely is a coincidence, I came across an ad in the newspaper. Headline: HOW MUCH MONEY SHOULD A MAN SPEND FOR A SUIT?

Did I read that ad, word for word? Did I learn what to look for, how much to pay, and where to get my new suit? You bet I did. In that case, as in most cases, marketing worked because it hit the target audience right between the eyes. I felt that ad was talking to me and not to some vague personage over my left shoulder.

Marketing could not have convinced me to buy a suit that week if I wasn't already thinking of buying one. But marketing that was geared to a person already in the market worked because it gave me exactly what I was looking for: information, benefits, and a place to make my purchase.

Those are the things I was really buying, and by providing them for me, Bullock & Jones won my business.

Marketing created a powerful desire in me to patronize that advertiser, and featured the reasons I really buy. That's why this golden rule suggests that yours should do the very same thing.

Solving Problems

Guerrilla Marketing's Golden Rule #4:
It is far easier to sell a solution to a problem than to sell a positive benefit.

FOR THIS REASON, guerrillas position their companies to be *problem-solvers*. They home in on the problems confronting their prospects, then offer their products and/or services as solutions to the problems.

Almost all companies are beset with problems of one sort or another. Your job, as a thinking guerrilla, is to spot those problems. One of the ways to do this is through networking. Networking is not a time to toot your own trombone, but to ask questions, listen attentively to the answers, and keep your marketing radar attuned to the presence of problems. Once you detect the problems, you can contact the prospect and talk about solutions. You can also discover problems that need solving by attending trade shows and professional association meetings and events, sending out prospect questionnaires, and making sales calls.

As you already know, people do not buy shampoo; they buy clean hair. That means selling a benefit. Some shampoo makers have boosted their profits by reassuring customers that their shampoo cleans hair *and solves the problem* of unmanageable hair — thereby offering a benefit *and a solution*.

Right now, products and services that are attaining the most success are those that help people quit smoking, lose weight, earn more money, improve health, grow (or give the appearance of growing) hair, eliminate wrinkles, and save time. These are problem-solving products and services.

Some of these products and services can also be positioned

Accentuate no positive; eliminate a negative

to accentuate a positive, but savvy company presidents instead stressed their capability to eliminate a negative. Your biggest job is to be sure your products and services do the same. Perhaps you'll have to undergo a major repositioning. That's not bad if it improves your profits. Far more doors will be open to you if you can achieve it.

Maybe you know right off what are the major problems facing your prospects. Your marketing should *highlight these problems*, then offer your product or service as the ideal solution. If you don't know the problems, knock yourself out learning about them. Regardless of the benefits you offer, the problems confronting a prospect almost always overshadow them.

It is not that difficult to position your offering as a problem-solver. But once you do, you'll find the task of marketing and selling becomes a whole lot easier in a hurry. Prospects don't

What prospects care about

care about *your company*; they care about *their problems*. If you can solve them, prospects will care about your company and want to buy what you are selling.

There's a good chance that you'll have to do some serious research to identify the problems of your customers. But a probing attitude is never resented if it is part of an attempt to spot and solve a problem. You may have to do extensive research to learn exactly what problems your product or service solves. A word of warning: don't claim to solve too many problems or your credibility will be undermined, and your primary focus will become blurred in the eyes of your prospects. Pick one problem that you solve especially well, then find prospects with this problem and present them with your solution.

A delightful aspect to positioning yourself as a problem-solver is that the job of locating prospects becomes that much easier. Those prospects are not on the lookout for your offering. But they are attuned to finding solutions to their problems. So all you have to do is feature the problem, secure in the knowledge that people who have it will respond to virtually anyone offering a solution. Do all people and all companies have problems? If you look long enough and hard enough, they do. And they'll be more than willing to discuss this problem with you — especially if you can do something about it.

Unfortunately, everybody has some sort of problem. Fortunately, your company can be geared to solve at least one of those problems. That's the way you've got to think. That's the mindset that must be conveyed by your marketing and by your representatives.

Guerrillas know that it often takes quite a bit of digging to uncover a problem. But they also know that if a problem exists in one place, it most likely exists in many. And they realize that if they can use case histories to show how a company or an individual suffered from a problem and how that problem is now solved, they can use these examples as steppingstones to a vital growth curve.

A powerful marketing plan mentions both the problem and the solution — to guide those who create marketing materials and prevent them from going off in the wrong direction. Sales training in guerrilla companies involves a discussion of problem-spotting, problem-discussing, and problem-solving. Sales reps learn the nature of prospect problems from one another. Sharing their insights helps the entire company.

Put the problem in your plan

Keep the concept of problem-solving alive in your mind, your marketing materials, your sales presentations, and your company mission. Be sure your employees are tuned into the same wavelength.

Strangely enough, as sensible as all this sounds, many companies are unaware of this rule for guerrilla marketers. They sell features. They sell benefits. But they neglect solutions because they have no radar for the problems faced by their prospects. Develop a radar for the prospect and offer solutions to problems customers may not even realize they have. This rule is so important to your business, it's golden.

The World's Best Customer List

Guerrilla Marketing's Golden Rule #5:
Your own customer list is the best in the world — but only if it bulges with information about each customer.

ORIENT YOUR MARKETING plan to capitalize upon the most valuable customer list in existence — your very own.

There's nothing like a good hot list of prospects who fit your target market right on the money. A list of prospects, primed to become customers, is exceeded in importance to you by only one other list — the one you kept from the first day you started in business. Or at least starting tomorrow. Your own customer list has a lot of things on it beyond mere names and addresses, if you're to think like a guerrilla.

As all guerrillas should know, it costs five times more to make a sale to a stranger than to an existing customer. In spite of that barefaced fact, many companies haven't gotten around to making a customer list. Operating without a customer list, a practice rampant among small businesses, is a strong indication you ought to think about going into another line of work.

Along with your customer list, brimming with useful information, you should maintain the aforementioned hot prospect list. Although it costs but one-fifth as much to sell to a customer, hot prospects are really customers waiting to be **Guerrillas are** born — and guerrillas are midwives.
midwives Harvey Mackay, author of *Swim with the Sharks Without Being Eaten Alive* (William Morrow & Company, New York, 1988), is also chairman of Mackay Envelope Corporation, which produces over 10 million envelopes each day. He knows

the value of every customer and key prospect, and so his customer list is loaded with details — *66 of them,* which should give you an idea of what a bound-for-glory customer list is all about.

Harvey and his salespeople know the education of the people on their list. They know about their customers' and key prospects' families. They're all filled in on the business background, even the office decor.

The Mackay Envelope Corporation moves those 10 million envelopes daily because its customer list provides its salespeople with details about their customers' lifestyles — which refers to smoking, drinking, eating, playing, driving, achieving, favorite sports teams, and other small but juicy details. Its customer list includes those nuggets of data among its 66 facts.

Can you imagine taking the time to gather all that information? *You'd better imagine taking that time.* That's part of the dues you pay to be a practicing guerrilla. If you don't want to pay them, be warned that even if you try to substitute media mega-money for in-depth research, the investment won't pay off as well.

Paying your dues

Harvey's company pays its dues and gains its customer and prospect data by devoting *time to personal contact.* It obtains more data from *other customers, suppliers, banks, newspapers, trade publications, reference librarians, television — and especially from receptionists, secretaries, telephone answerers, and assistants of many varieties.* Information doesn't care where it comes from.

Once you have the information you seek, *the sales reps who contact the customers and prospects on your list must commit that data to memory or it may be wasted.* You should hold a seminar on the new service customers said they wanted to learn about on the questionnaire; mail personal letters to the prospects whose questionnaires show they can benefit soonest from doing business with you; take a large group of baseball-loving customers and prospects to a ballgame — just so you form a closer bond with them. You *know* a baseball game is a winner with these good people because your research told you so.

Don't take all of your customers and prospects to these special events — only those who are especially hot prospects, especially good customers, or exceptionally high rollers in terms of buying big ticket items from you. Extravagant service should be extended to all customers and prospects. But with some of these people, an extra measure of extravagant service may be a wise investment. Because you know what these folks like, you know exactly where to make that investment so that it hits home the most.

Use the information you've gathered in conversation, direct mail, faxes, notes, phone calls, answering machine and voice mail messages, modem communication — wherever you can. You can be certain that your prospect has never witnessed such a caring attitude and so much proven personal attention. In gathering the information, you have already devoted much of the herculean effort necessary to generate a repeat sale to a customer and convert a prospect to a customer.

The most important person you've met

If I were to take a guess as to the most important person you've ever met, I'd guess that it was any one of your customers. That person, if treated well, will make repeat purchases and will refer folks to your business. The larger and more detailed your customer list, the less you have to invest in expensive mass marketing.

Your customers have identified themselves to you, and that makes it a cinch to identify yourself to them. Keep in touch with them. Make them feel as if they have "joined your club." Take my word, ordinary businesspeople do not exert as much intensive customer energy. Guerrillas do.

The L. L. Bean Company, famed for mail order success, excellent merchandise, and superb service, tells employees

- A customer is the most important person ever in this office, in person, or by mail.
- A customer is not dependent on us; we are dependent on him.
- A customer is not an interruption of our work; he is the purpose of it. We are not doing a favor by serving him; he is doing us a favor by giving us the opportunity to do so.

- A customer is not someone to argue or match wits with. Nobody ever won an argument with a customer.
- A customer is a person who brings us his wants. It is our job to handle them profitably to him and to ourselves.

Keep your customer list current, because experts warn that if your data is older than 90 days, chances are it is already becoming out-of-date. This is not as hard as it sounds if you commit to tracking customers as they change, meeting with them in person, and being sure to visit them on their turf. Enlist everyone in your company as a data-gatherer. Subscribe to all the trade publications. The information is out there. All you've got to do is get it — usually for free. It's ironic that the key to success — customer relations — is free for the taking. **It must be up-to-date**

The key is free

What you're doing when you act upon your information is *making the customer feel important*. To enhance the feeling of customer importance, give each customer access to you personally by means of a direct phone line. Don't blow this dialogue tool with an officious secretary.

Computers make it easier than ever to maintain customer lists with fresh information. The compiling and maintenance of a customer list is one of the guerrilla's most crucial chores. Be sure you do it or delegate it to someone who will do it as well as Harvey Mackay.

A proper customer list is another marketing art form. In the hands of the guerrilla, it is a sighting scope to bull's-eyes. When your list has all of the details necessary to prove beyond doubt that your personal attention exceeds that of any other company, it will be the world's best customer list. And you will be the beneficiary of this golden rule.

Customer Reverence

Guerrilla Marketing's Golden Rule #6:
Consistently display your reverence for your customers by trying to help them with consistent follow-up.

A CUSTOMER IS a very special person. Of the billions of people on planet Earth, only a tiny fraction have chosen to do business with you. They have selected your business on purpose. It is your constant obligation — though it should be a pleasure — to do what you can to improve the lives of these people: with valuable advice, with reduced prices, with previews of new products and services.

The only way to do it is by staying in touch, by breaking down the barriers of apathy — on your part and theirs. Every guerrilla knows that 80 percent of business lost in America is lost not due to high prices or poor service, but because of apathy after the sale. And what's the opposite of apathy? You've got it — customer reverence.

The opposite of apathy

Guerrillas demonstrate their customer reverence in a variety of ways. Consider some or all of these fifteen as starters:

1. A thank-you note within 48 hours of the purchase, although 24 hours is even more impressive and memorable. Anyone can send a thank-you note. Guerrillas do it ASAP.

2. An offer of an item related to their purchase, tendered about 30 days after the purchase. The offer can be for a product or a service. If you don't have the ideal follow-up offering, team up in a strategic alliance with someone who does. Not seeing this as the future of American business means you're facing in the wrong direction.

3. A questionnaire mailed about three months after your first contact. You'll use it to gain more than the standard in-

formation if you're like the major cellular phone company that actually studies the handwriting on the questionnaire for insights into the respondent's personality. Handwriting analysis is not a science, but it can be a valuable guide. The more you understand your customers, the better you can practice customer reverence.

4. A birthday card, easy to send after you've sent the questionnaire and learned the birthday — month and day, not year. Later you can expand this tactic to send graduation cards to the customer's kids, anniversary cards to the customer and spouse, and as a business owner who is heartset on being a guerrilla, postcards from your next vacation. Don't overwhelm your customers, but continue to acknowledge their existence. This highly personal approach is not for all of your customers, but for the long-term, loyal, large purchaser, the kind who occasionally recommends your business to others. This tactic is not for oil companies, utilities, and leaders in the *Fortune* 500. But it's dynamite for almost any small business or professional with a roster of anywhere from three to 100 key customers. Heck, even the *Fortune* 500 can use it in this way.

5. A telemarketing offer, made when it is most convenient to your customer — which you learned from the questionnaire. The conversation should be warm and cozy. Brief, too. The person called should be immediately identified as an appreciated customer.

6. A newsletter, sent monthly, bimonthly, or quarterly. If it's created with customer reverence in mind, it will give more than it asks, provide valuable free information, and still make offers to sell something. Newsletters are fertile grounds for fusion marketing arrangements. You recommend AT&T in your newsletter and they recommend you in theirs. Or some similar arrangement.

7. A customer contest, guaranteed to be won by a customer and not some bozo who has not yet discovered your offerings. Inform customers that their odds are better in your contest than in the state lottery because, alas, your customer list is smaller than the state population.

8. A request for referrals. It should be straightforward, honest, and reasonable in asking customers for the names of only three people or companies that could benefit by doing business with you.

9. A preferred-customer show at which new models or styles are previewed. Customers are under no pressure to buy and are made to feel privileged at seeing things first. At such an event, refreshments are a must.

10. A secret sale with discounts that are available to customers and only to customers. Naturally, this cannot be supported with mass market advertising. But it's okay with you if the customer brings a friend.

11. A time-limited offer that is revealed to your customers first and to the general public in exactly one week. This does the double duty of treating customers in a special manner while hastening their purchase.

12. A fact-of-interest postcard. This is sent in the purest sense of customer reverence because it gives data that can help your customer and does not try to sell anything. Keep it brief, and customers will actually look forward to your mailings, a dream world for most, but the standard situation for guerrillas.

13. An audio or video brochure, depending upon the size of your profit per sale. The audio brochure will run under $1 each, while the video brochure can go for five times that amount. Never send these to strangers; try to send them to the customers you revere.

14. A catalogue of your offerings, sent only to customers if you have enough, or sent first to customers, then to prospects if your customer list isn't long enough. Customers will especially appreciate a catalogue clearly communicating that it is for customers only.

15. A special offer made on the anniversary of the exact date that the customer made that all-important first purchase. Have you ever received such an offer? Only if you patronize guerrillas. That's why such a tactic will help you stand out from the other capitalists.

If you don't stay in contact with your customer, somebody else will woo that rare person away from you. On a constant basis, you must fan the flames of love and loyalty. This will prove beyond any words that you practice customer reverence, an automatic safeguard against apathy.

Forever fan the flames

Why do you suppose all evidence proves that it costs five times as much to sell to a new customer as to an existing customer? That's easy. Because the price is high to find a new customer while the price is free to find an existing customer. It's far less expensive to get a subscriber to renew a magazine subscription than to attract a new subscriber.

That's why customer reverence makes so much sense. Guerrillas stay in touch with their customers, more and more customers with each marketing effort. This has the effect, over time, of constantly increasing your profits while reducing your marketing investment. It embodies the spirit of guerrilla marketing because it relies upon your imagination and energy instead of your bank account.

The guerrilla spirit

Customer reverence is felt by the heart and planned by the mind. It is proved with mailings, calls, gifts, savings, information, anything to benefit the customer. When you prove it, repeat and referral sales are your just and generous rewards for following this golden rule.

Convenience

Design your business to operate for the convenience of your customers, and make it very easy to do business with you.

ALTHOUGH IT HAS always been important to offer convenience, it is more important now than ever because of the growing realization in America of *the elusive nature of time.*

Practitioners of guerrilla marketing see that as a clear signal that, now more than ever, people do not like waiting around, do not like difficulty in making a purchase, do not like doing business with companies that waste their time, do not want companies to dawdle with their orders or fail to render instant service. For many people, instant gratification is not quite fast enough.

The large majority of people want to lead a more streamlined life. As a guerrilla, you've got to cater to their goal.

The public's recognition of time's importance so directly affects marketing that I've added an additional point to my original "eight words ending with *ent*" so that I could include *convenient.* That's how crucial it is to successful marketing.

The guerrilla's new credo The guerrilla's credo is now: commitment, investment, consistent, confident, patient, assortment, subsequent, amazement, and *convenient.* These concepts are explained in greater detail in *Guerrilla Marketing* and *Guerrilla Marketing Attack.*

Bend over backward offering convenience to your prospects and customers. Here are ten ways to make it easy for people to do business with you. The more of these customer conveniences you put into practice, the more you can profit.

1. Do what you must to enable prospects and customers to make purchases from you *seven days a week.*

2. Take the necessary steps for those same precious humans to buy from you *24 hours a day.* Need some convincing? Ask the owners of 7-Eleven, Safeway, or Wells Fargo Bank armored services.

3. Accept *as many credit cards as you can.* I know that many people have the two big credit cards. But a lot of them are at the limit, so honor the other credit cards, too.

4. Let your customers pay with *partial payment plans.* Break the total tab into three, six, or twelve easy payments. The lower the number, the higher the number of sales, even if the total isn't a low number.

5. Offer the convenience of a *toll-free phone number.* You can use it to handle inquiries, take orders, render service. Experts claim it increases responses by 30 percent. You don't need a toll-free number if you're dealing with local people only. Those people want to know where to find you so they can punch you in the nose if your product poops out on them.

6. Publish a *catalogue or brochure* so that prospects and customers have easy access to data about your products right in their files or at their fingertips.

7. Take pains to be sure your order forms and invoices are *written clearly and understandably.* While you're at it, see to it that your *lighting is bright,* that your *parking is ample,* and that you can *fax information* to potential buyers who might also want to be able to fax orders to you.

8. If you must put customers on hold after they telephone, let them listen to *special offerings and news* about your company while they are waiting. Don't waste their time. A full 85 percent will continue listening to your on-hold message.

9. Examine all aspects of your business, and although they should be geared to quality and profitability, be sure they also are *oriented to speed.* If you're fast in five areas and slow in the sixth, that one bottleneck may erode your reputation for convenience.

10. Do whatever you can to say "yes" to every question posed by a prospect or customer. While it will be impossible in 100 percent of the cases, it is possible in 75 percent. The more you can say "yes," the easier you are to buy from.

As more and more people value their time, those same people will begin doing business with companies that are openly oriented to customer convenience in every aspect of their operation. Even if you have long-standing relationships **Why customers** with customers, don't be surprised if these good people desert **may desert you** you for another company that offers more convenience and saves more of their time.

Just a decade ago, most Americans resented answering devices and grimaced when their phone calls to a business were answered by a machine. Today — and in the years ahead — people *appreciate* the convenience of an answering technology, be it voice-mail, an answering service, or a voice-activated machine that can take long messages.

These people are grateful that they can phone in the middle of the night and place their entire order, or lodge their complaint. Where Puritan principles created a system of commerce that closed down on Sundays, humanistic principles motivate today's businesses to remain open on Sundays because it is a convenient day to shop.

Visit successful businesses and see if they are offering any conveniences that you're not offering. See if they're doing anything that you're not doing to save the customers' time. Ask your customers what you can do to provide more convenience. You can be sure they'll tell you, and you can profit from the information.

Enlist the aid of your employees in your quest for the ulti-**Think like a** mate in convenience. Think like a customer, not a business **customer** owner. Think of the businesses that you patronize and whether they offer any conveniences that attracted you.

If you have customer convenience on your mind, you'll consider delivering, doing business at your customer's place instead of your own, encouraging phone orders, establishing a mail-order system, adding service reps, and providing shuttle service for customers. I've been patronizing the same auto service garage for over 20 years. They keep me happy by having my car ready on time and coming in with final prices beneath their estimates.

But they won my business in the first place because they offered to drive me home when I dropped off my car and to pick me up when it had been serviced. I have a client who runs a printing and copying business and picks up and delivers 95 percent of his orders. He takes great satisfaction knowing that most of his competition doesn't even offer pickup and delivery. No wonder his is the largest operation of its kind in the area.

The business world has evolved to the point where convenience is an art form as well as an advanced technology. The **An art form** day has already come when customers can purchase from television data, then order and pay by telephone. The golden rule concerning convenience is alive, well, and gaining stature every day.

The Power of Questions

Guerrilla Marketing's Golden Rule #8:
Questions lead to answers; answers lead to customer rapport; customer rapport leads to profits.

THERE IS A FREE, potent, and multipurpose guerrilla marketing weapon that many companies can, but do not use. Or they use it, but obtain only a fraction of what it can offer. To gain rapport with your customers and data that can make or break your company — be sure you know both the power of questions and the many insights you can gain from the answers to those questions.

Mirrors of the mind   The answers to your questions are mirrors of your customers' minds. To fully comprehend the significance of this, consider three basic truths:

1. The more customer rapport, the more profits.
2. Information empowers your marketing.
3. Handwriting can give clues to personality.

By combining the truths in those fundamental but seemingly unrelated facts, you can develop the kind of rapport with your customers that leads to more repeat business, larger orders, and solid referral business. To be sure we're on the same track, because this is very important to many businesses, let's take a moment to check the three basics.

Rapport is defined as a "harmonious or sympathetic relationship." If you have this kind of relationship, your customer treats you like a partner and friend. You treat your customer the same way. You really are partners. You really are friends. You want to help your customer and you know just how to do it — because you've asked questions, paid close attention to the answers, and built rapport. As every guerrilla knows, confidence leads to more sales than any other single factor, and as any guerrilla can surmise, rapport builds confidence.

Information lets you know what your customer needs. It is not always what your customer wants. Focusing sharply on those needs and obtaining the customer's agreement that he or she does need those things enables you to tailor your products, services, and marketing to the customer's real needs. From your brochures to your sales calls, everything is centered on those needs. You learn these needs by asking questions, by analyzing the answers (not merely reading or listening to them), and by gaining crucial information. The more information you have, the greater rapport you can build.

Questions reveal needs

Handwriting is widely recognized as a clue to character. The practice of handwriting analysis, called graphology, is used by large corporations to screen personnel, by lawyers to select jurors, and by psychiatrists to gain a more comprehensive view of their patients. It is admissible in court as evidence and is not at all connected with the pseudoscientific fields of astrology, palm-reading, and seances. This concept of *analyzing answers and handwriting* is right up any guerrilla's alley — because it is nontraditional, unconventional, effective, and new. It's so new I didn't even include it in *Guerrilla Marketing Weapons*. Such is the ever changing nature of marketing. As I mentioned earlier, one of the nation's leading cellular phone companies trains its sales force in handwriting as it relates to marketing.

A new weapon

The immense power of questions is revealed by answers to inquiries such as

- What are the three best things about our company?
- What are the three worst things about our company?
- If you could create an ideal company in our industry, how would it differ from ours?
- Which three U.S. companies do you respect the most?

Questions guerrillas ask

Your job now is to determine what customer information you want so that you can design the most effective questionnaire.

Then be prepared to act upon the data you gain. If you're not responsive to the answers, what's the purpose of the exercise? The power of questions is the power of answers . . . and what you do with them.

Most companies don't even send out customer questionnaires. Some send out the questionnaires and study the answers, but ignore the handwriting. Guerrillas, in their efforts to use as much science as possible in their marketing, ask the questions, study the answers, analyze the handwriting, then style their presentations to fit both the needs *and* the personality of their customers and prospects. When my clients send out long questionnaires to their customers, they are always startled at the high rate of response. People appreciate being recognized for their expertise, and nobody is as expert on customers as a real-life customer.

If you're going to ask a lot of questions, explain why you're doing so. Here's how a home meal-delivery service might do it:

We're starting up a new service that delivers dinners right to your home or apartment. You can order the meals from any of five restaurants on the menu we supply, then call us direct and we'll have the food to you within one hour. So that we can be of maximum service, we'd appreciate it if you would take a moment to answer these questions. Thank you!

How many people live in your home or apartment? _____
What are their ages? _____
Who usually prepares dinner where you live? _____
How often do you eat out? _____
What are the three main benefits of having dinner delivered to your home?

    1. _____
    2. _____
    3. _____

Would you pay a $5 delivery fee for this service? _____
What is your sex? _____Your household income? _____
What newspapers do you read? _____

What radio stations do you listen to? _____

What TV shows do you watch? _____

Do you have cable TV? _____Satellite dish? _____

What magazines do you read? _____

What type of work do you do? _____

How many working adults live in your home? _____

What are your favorite types of cuisine? _____

Why would you not use our service? _____

Where would you expect us to advertise? _____

Do you have any other comments or advice? _____

We're grateful for your time and will try to make it up to you with tasty, hot dinners that will save you time.

One of the most winning aspects of questions is not simply their power, but their economy. It costs nothing to come up with the questions. It costs very little to print questionnaires. It costs zero to obtain the names of your customers. It costs hardly anything to mail the questionnaires to them.

That's why following this golden rule is the essence of guerrilla marketing — a big bang for itsy-bitsy bucks.

The Perils of Showtime

Guerrilla Marketing's Golden Rule #9:
Marketing is always more effective if it is looked upon as
selltime rather than showtime.

GUERRILLAS LOVE SHOWS. They attend theater. They go to
concerts. You can find them following the libretto at the opera
or matching wits with contestants on television game shows.
They even sob during soaps. They enjoy being entertained
and many of them do a sterling job of entertaining.

But they know where to draw the line between showtime
and selltime. They know deep in their hearts that *marketing*
time is not showtime. And they know that they must forever

The irresistible
allure

resist the temptation to fall into showtime, the irresistible allure of show business, the siren song of an enthralled audience, and the pressure from wet-behind-the-ears colleagues to
transform selltime into showtime. It is not all that easy to be
a guerrilla. You've got to get your kicks from honest profits
rather than roaring crowds.

When you create a marketing weapon, you are a salesperson, not a showperson. You want sales and profits, not ap-
plause and awards. You also want the people who read your
materials to get enough information to want your products and
services enough to buy them. So your job is to *provide that*
information while creating a desire to buy what you sell.

Knowing this, you can be as entertaining as you want, en-
casing and surrounding your offering with as much glitz and
glamour as you want — just as long as the glitz and the glamour don't get in the way of your response rates. To be sure,
marketing must capture attention and arouse interest if it's
to be noticed, let alone motivate people to purchase your
offering.

Although you have my permission to be as clever and witty and entertaining as a clown parade, you have my warning that any trace of cleverness runs the risk of getting in the way of your basic message. This is true of cleverness, humor, art, and all the other scene-stealers that have caused innocent business owners to waste billions of marketing dollars. Billions may be an understatement.

A permission and a warning

Showtime, which is the first aim of the imagination-impoverished, should instead be the technique of last resort. People tend to create the showtime, then stick in the product or service if they can make it fit. Guerrillas create powerful selling ideas, then set up an atmosphere of showtime with the idea as the star. And most of the time they walk away from showtime altogether. No, let me amend that: they run away.

Given the chance, your readers, viewers, and prospects will remember the showtime glitter and not the marketing idea, even if it was a gem. Once you have the attention of your prospects, you don't want to waste it with cutie-pie words, distracting graphics, and memorable humor — memorable at the expense of your offering.

Once you have that oh-so-dear attention, direct it to win a share of your readers' and viewers' and listeners' minds. Convey the winning identity of your offering. Stress your benefits, your uniqueness, your desirability. Aim your message to one person at a time rather than a throng waiting to be entertained. And ask for action. The action you want is not a guffaw but a purchase. Not a belly laugh but an order. There's a time for laughing and a time for earning honest profits.

No time for laughing

The perils of showtime are also in the expectations of business owners, marketing creators, and the media. This means that although showtime almost always upstages selltime, people think that marketing and showtime fit together like ham and eggs when the truth is they don't fit together at all.

But marketing audiences have been conditioned to look for showtime during selltime. After all, other companies give them a good laugh, why not your company? Instead of looking for the idea in your offering, they're looking for the show.

Your uphill battle is to keep them happy with your offering *by making it the show.*

Showtime is expensive to produce, tempting to run in the media, fun to watch, and easy to love. But is it marketing? Not at all. Is it guerrilla marketing? Hardly. Guerrillas get all their entertainment from their profit-and-loss statements. They create marketing that causes people to say "I want that product!" rather than "I liked that commercial!"

With more dazzling special effects available in both print and electronic media, there is more than ever to resist. But resist it you must. Force yourself. Before approving any marketing material for production, reread this chapter.

You never want to kid your customers and prospects. Need I tell you that you also must never kid yourself? If you're wooed by showtime and tend toward inserting it in your marketing, perhaps you do need the warning. Right now, at this moment, I know that you agree with the wisdom of this golden rule. But there's no business like show business, and when you find yourself attracted to the flame, it's easy to forget how badly you can get burned.

Don't let that happen! If you think that marketing is a jungle, showtime is a minefield. It has blown up many a great idea, caused many a company to go into bankruptcy. With such high stakes and serious consequences, you must adhere to the guerrilla's irrefutable avoidance of showtime. Besides, showtime can never be as much bottom-line fun as selltime. Follow this golden rule and tell me which gives you the most enjoyment after you've made your first bank deposit.

Introducing New Products and Services

Guerrilla Marketing's Golden Rule #10:
When introducing new offerings, enthusiastically announce that they're new and clearly explain why they're good.

JUST AS WITH first impressions, you get only one chance to introduce a new product or service, and that introduction will influence the opinions of many people for a long time. So you've got to do everything possible with that introduction to make the right impression on the right people. In your mind, underline *right impression* and *right people*. Guerrillas give these matters deep thought.

There are many impressions that you will make with your introductory marketing. About half are the wrong impression and half are the right impression. If you use the mindset of your target audience when you consider the impression, you'll probably avoid making the wrong impression. That's half the battle and it's not the easy half.

Your product or service need not be the best, the cheapest, or the most modern. But it must be exactly what your hottest prospects want. And you've got to communicate that fact in an unmistakable manner.

No need to be best

Out there in your target market, there are people who become bewitched and captivated by anything that is new. They purchase products and services simply because they are new. These are the *Yes-to-New People*: turned on by innovation. Some markets are like that, too. In the women's shampoo market, 90 percent of the customers will try at least one new shampoo a year. New is more powerful than lather in shampoo language. Brand loyalty is hard to come by.

Mixed in with these try-anything-new folks is the wait-and-see crowd. They're the *No-to-New People*. They don't buy certain things solely because they're new. They distrust anything they haven't heard of, even if it's demonstrably better. Why? Because they don't cotton to strangers. And if you're new, **An automatic** you're an automatic stranger.
stranger

Your marketing should be aimed and worded for the *Maybe-to-New People*. Luckily, that describes the majority of the human race anyhow.

The Yes-to-New group within your target market will buy what you sell because it is new. That's all they need to know. Don't waste your money convincing them; they don't need convincing.

The No-to-New group in your audience will not buy what you sell because it is new. That's all they need to know. Don't waste your money convincing them; they can't be convinced — not yet at least.

Happily, the big chunk of your audience wants to know more than the mere fact that your product or service is new. They want to know why it's good, and they're wide-open to the reasons they should own it. They'll pay attention to what your marketing has to say if it interests them, but you've got to roll up your sleeves to get them to buy it. But realize this: *they want to buy it.*

Ten guerrilla   Here are ten guerrilla hints to make that happen.
hints

1. Aim your marketing and your message only to the maybes and not one iota to the yeses or nos.
2. Show your confidence in your product or service by the way you introduce it. Tell why new makes it better.
3. In your marketing materials, use the words *new, announcing, introducing, first of its kind,* and *finally.* Convey the feeling of a breakthrough. But be careful not to exaggerate and undermine your credibility.
4. After the bugs have been worked out and distribution is set, fire your big guns. Run big ads. Do direct mail that's coordinated with other direct marketing methods.

For example, combining television and telemarketing may work well.

5. Be certain there is a cohesiveness in your ads, brochures, sales presentations, letters, postcards, logo, claims, theme, and everything else on the marketing front.

6. Use testimonials from your pioneer users as soon as possible. Quote specific lines. Use specific numbers. This will dramatically speed you toward your goal.

7. As soon as possible, talk community acceptance or industry acceptance. Show how others just like those in your target market are already benefiting from your doodad.

8. Be certain that your publicity is in sync with your other marketing, appearing right at the outset but not too early. Better a month late than a month early. Use reprints of that publicity in your other marketing efforts.

9. Convey a spirit of excitement in your copy, in your sales force, in your marketing. Enthusiasm works all the time, but is best at the launch when it's needed the most.

10. Know what you will do with your marketing after the honeymoon is over. New is new for six months at most and you may break the bank during that time. But you must make a change. Set up that change with your introductory marketing, having phase two lurking in the copy. When you're ready, you'll be glad you planned for the change. Even after phase two has been launched, be prepared with the campaign that will follow — even though it might be three years before it sees the light of day. The idea is to avoid emergencies by being ready to go, but restrained enough to know when to go.

After the honeymoon

The introductory period is a rare and crucial time in the life of a product or service. For many of them, it is the key to success or failure.

Introducing new products and services is a special art, quite different from standard marketing. In the hands of a guerrilla, it is a precious opportunity to earn hefty profits. The setbacks of a poorly coordinated new product or service introduction often take years to overcome, if, indeed, they can be overcome at all. The momentum established by a hot and vital introductory period lasts for years and can be built upon to generate profits even with a vastly reduced marketing budget.

Spend up to 50 percent of the annual budget for your three-month introduction. Spread the rest out over the remainder of **The two musts**   the year. Two musts: spend a giant chunk of your budget to introduce your offerings, and leave enough to continue promoting it the rest of the year.

You're a sprinter, crouched in the starting position, feet on the starting blocks, leaning forward to leap ahead at the sound of the starter's gun. Do you need me to tell you the need for a good start? This golden rule rewards you with a lead over your competitors in the race and in the market.

Sources of Marketing Know-how

Guerrilla Marketing's Golden Rule #11:
The more know-how you have about the overall marketing process, the more profits you will earn.

MOST PEOPLE ARE intimidated by marketing, even those who practice it for a living or are dependent upon it for survival. To defuse that intimidation and minimize costly marketing errors, it makes sense to gain the maximum amount of marketing information on a continual basis. Knowledge is the power that fuels marketing. Know-how is a major competitive advantage.

The power that fuels marketing

Combined with know-how, insight is a crucial factor in productive marketing. This guerrilla's dictionary defines insight as "the capacity to discern the true nature of a thing, especially through intuitive understanding." This is not to say that marketing is dictated by gut reactions and knee-jerk instincts. Common sense should defeat intuition every time. But insight gives you intuition, and if you have both common sense in the way of know-how and intuition in the way of insight, you're equipped to do battle and to win.

With this insight and marketing know-how, you may not be able to create great marketing, but you *will* know the difference between great and gruesome marketing. Knowing the difference will have a potent impact on your profit-and-loss statement.

Of the several methods of gaining marketing know-how, and you're engaged in one of them now — reading a book about marketing — probably the most enlightening is life experience. I say "probably" because real life teaches some people and goes over the heads of others.

Where to find insights

Reading marketing books gives you valuable insights. And

there are more excellent books on the topic than ever before. I'm not talking about textbooks or volumes devoted to companies with megamillion budgets. Instead, I'm suggesting that you browse the shelves of good bookstores in search of marketing insight.

Superb seminars on marketing are also available, many through university extensions, many more through entrepreneurial organizations. You'll discover that some of these seminars provide overviews of marketing, some are highly specialized in certain aspects of it, and others are sleeves-up, hands-on experiences.

Then, of course, there are the marketing magazines. Of all of them, the one I like best these days is *Adweek*. You can subscribe with a toll-free call to 1-800-722-6658.

Although *Adweek* is loaded with industry gossip, you can skip those pages and go right to the know-how sections where they report on marketing advancements and conduct in-depth investigations into marketing trends.

I'll admit that three weeks out of four, you'll find the trends and ideas fascinating and enjoyable to read, but they won't do diddly for your company. Still, one week out of four, you'll come across a marketing concept that you can immediately put to use.

The marketing ploy might be one that worked wonders in Florence, Italy, or Fort Lauderdale, Florida. You don't care where it came from. All you need is the marketing insight it provides you. And it never hurts if you gain an extra dollop of creativity from the idea. This is not to suggest that you copy the idea, only that you become inspired by it.

A treasury of marketing know-how   A treasury of marketing books appears in the bibliography of *Finding Your Niche . . . Marketing Your Professional Service* by Bart Brodsky and Janet Geis (Community Resource Institute Press, 1992, Berkeley, CA, 510-525-9663). Many supply the exact know-how you need right now. Any guerrilla seeking enlightenment has a copy in his or her office and more than a few of the books on his or her bookshelf.

Newsletters on marketing can also illuminate your way. You're going to need all the illumination you can get during the 1990s when marketing competition is fiercer than ever, more companies than ever are vying for *your* customers' dollars, and marketing victories come only to companies possessed of the most know-how and the deepest insight.

Unlike many fields that can be learned by intense study, marketing is an ever-changing industry, transforming from an art to a science as you read this. New media are popping up all over the place. People are experimenting and either falling flat on their faces or achieving new highs in profits. Learn from these experiences. Marketing know-how keeps you abreast of these changes. It can make the difference between success and failure.

At all times, the most crucial know-how to have is the basic way that marketing works and doesn't work. These golden rules have been formulated and published to increase the breadth of your know-how and to impart insight.

Insight occurs when marketing sheds its mystique and you see clearly the steps of the process. Only after you have gone through that process will you gain the perspective to see that marketing is simple unless *you* make it complicated. Many business owners have, cumulatively, lost literally billions of dollars because they never gained any insight into marketing — any workable know-how. When working with marketing professionals, smart business owners see to it that the professionals teach as they act, showing the business owner how to be comfortable around marketing, indeed, how to create profitable marketing.

No more marketing mystique

When there are 100 businesses operating in a community and all 100 are invited to attend a marketing seminar, why is it that only 25 will attend? Because the other 75 think that marketing is either too complex or not applicable to their business. This is a happy situation for any guerrilla — for the guerrilla wishes to keep insights private, to keep marketing know-how within her province only. No self-respecting guerrillas want their competitors to know how to use marketing. Do you want yours to know these golden rules?

Guerrilla know-how differs from standard marketing know-how because it relies less on money and more on knowing how to best use time, energy, and imagination. Guerrilla know-how reveals a bountiful arsenal of weaponry that may be used to wage and win marketing wars. Guerrilla know-how lets guerrillas know exactly what to do when they are copied.

Successful marketing almost always gets copied by those with less fertile imaginations. The neophyte throws up his hands in despair. But the guerrilla knew the copying would happen, takes it in stride, and moves on to phase two of the guerrilla marketing plan.

Of the providers of continuing marketing know-how I've seen, the most valuable, he said without even a shred of modesty, is *The Guerrilla Marketing Newsletter*, at $49 per year in the U.S. and available by calling 1-800-748-6444 or sending your check to Guerrilla Marketing International, 260 Cascade Drive, Box 1336, Mill Valley, CA 94942. I admit *that* is advertising. I also guarantee that it will provide valuable benefits to you, benefits worth far more than $49.

**Call
1-800-748-6444**

Marketing is too important to your business to be practiced in the dark. That's why the rule is to gain the most possible guerrilla know-how — and never stop adding to it.

Honesty

Do everything in your power to employ marketing techniques and tactics that are honest beyond reproach.

THERE IS NO QUESTION that there is honesty in marketing. But people don't believe that statement. Do you?

A national poll revealed that 53 percent of the American population sense a "feeling of deception" about marketing. Even you and I have always known that when it comes to marketing, the American public has a built-in B.S. detector. Advertising people rank fairly low on the credibility scale.

A small, but growing number of marketing practitioners have created the impression of deceit. Most marketing is honest in that it tells the truth. But a great deal of marketing exaggerates, primarily due to enthusiasm on the part of the company and the copywriter. The line between exaggeration and dishonesty is a hazy one. But once you've crossed it, it's hard to go back and regain your customer's trust. Guerrillas avoid stepping over that line.

Although I cannot claim that honesty is one of the most valuable weapons in the arsenal of a guerrilla (although it should be in every arsenal), I can advise you that dishonesty is one of the mortal enemies of your reputation and your marketing. Dishonesty detracts from your offering, from the media in general, and from all marketing efforts. To be perfectly candid, it is very difficult to be believed in the marketing environment in the first place, even when you tell the truth. You've got to bend over backward to be believed.

One way to gain belief is to admit a failing from the past. Another way is to find something about your company that is not the best, but not important — then admit that fault. Everything you say after that will be believed because you have been honest in admitting a weakness or flaw.

One of my favorite guerrillas, owner of a large chain of video rental stores, requires that all employees select a movie that they dislike so, that they can warn customers about it. Again, everything they say after that will be believed because they have established their credibility. They won't try to sell you *everything*.

Hype is all around us

It's too bad that you've got to take measures to establish your honesty in the buyer's mind, but the level of hype most consumers have come to take for granted has made that a marketing reality.

A more positive way to gain credibility is to publish a newsletter or give a seminar, lending to your authority, hence your expertise. Frequent advertising with consistent back-up on the variety of claims — discounts, purchase incentives — all combine to give the consumer an aura of trust. What's worse, after all, than making a special trip to a store only to find the "as advertised" discounted item out of stock? Most consumers would interpret that as a ruse and lose faith in your business credibility.

It is quite simple to be honest in all of your marketing. It is quite difficult to be believed. Your statements must have the ring of truth and the feeling of sincerity. But they can't sound patronizing. You've got to be conscious of those who surround you in the pages or on the airwaves. They may be spouting lies like there's no tomorrow. Use believable words and phrases. Advertising legend Leo Burnett termed it "shirt-sleeve English." Although a single honest marketing weapon

Proving your honesty

won't prove your honesty, your continued reverence of truth in marketing will.

Marketing that is 99 percent honest and 1 percent dishonest will have the dishonesty exposed and held up to the spotlight, if not to the piercing questions of *60 Minutes*. People will tend to believe your marketing based upon their unconscious assessment of your *most unbelievable statement*. That means you can undo a dynamite marketing program with one clinker.

For as long as marketing exists, it will be perceived by a skeptical public as possibly spurious. The public will take your most heartfelt statements with a grain of salt. This is not your fault. But it is your obligation to surmount that obstacle. And it is also your obligation to do nothing to increase the height of the obstacle.

As a rule of thumb, keep in mind that almost every descriptive adjective in your copy detracts from the feeling of honesty. Use facts instead of opinions. Use specific numbers rather than vague allusions to numbers. Use names, dates, and places, when possible, to add to the feeling of honesty in your marketing.

Think of it this way: if you were writing a newspaper article, it really wouldn't matter how honest you were. People have the notion going-in that honesty and factual truth are preconditions of the form.

But when you are coming up to bat and your goal is success at marketing, you have two strikes against you the moment you step up to the plate. This means your job is not going to be easy; it's going to be harder than the job of a novelist. Even Ernest Hemingway admitted that writing advertising is a far more difficult discipline than writing fiction. Fiction is supposed to be inventive and is viewed as a work of imagination, even gross exaggeration. Marketing is supposed to be fact, but unfortunately is viewed as fiction. **Two strikes against you**

It is obvious that your marketing should be honest. But if it really were that obvious, the public would believe marketing. And they don't. Blame this negative attitude on the countless fast-talking hucksters who have come before you. They've dug a deep hole. That hole is your starting point.

Your task is to climb out of that hole. Examine every iota of your marketing to see if you've succeeded. Is every sentence blatantly honest? Does every word ring with the truth? Is your company theme believable or the same old puffery the others are practicing? What about your visuals? Do the models look

No phoniness allowed phony? Are they smiling in situations where people don't ordinarily smile? Or are your visuals so unreal that they automatically set off the disbelief alarms?

Pretend that the world's biggest cynic sits atop your right shoulder. Every time you create a marketing piece, listen to that cynic. The cynic is there to keep you on the straight and narrow, making sure that everything looks and sounds on the up-and-up and that you are following this golden rule.

Profits

Guerrilla Marketing's Golden Rule #13:
Everything in your marketing should be designed to increase your profits, not merely your sales, but your profits.

IT'S AXIOMATIC in marketing that "it's not creative unless it moves merchandise." Moving merchandise is not a bad thing, to be sure, but if you don't earn a healthy profit when it moves, you're missing the point of being in business.

Missing the point

But alas, not all companies think that way. They make dire errors in the good name of marketing. Let's be clear right at the outset that marketing is supposed to earn profits.

Marketing is not supposed to create sales at the expense of profits, speed up turnover at the expense of profits, or generate traffic at the expense of profits.

If you're getting the idea that marketing's only true measurement is profits, you're pretty close to getting it right. But as mass communication, marketing is part of the evolutionary process, as well as a business's evolutionary process, and as such, it has an obligation not to offend, not to be in poor taste, not to be insensitive, and not to lie. Keeping that in mind *plus* understanding that the obligation of marketing is to generate profits, you've got a good handle on the role of marketing.

Some companies discount their products and services so much that they attract a lot of traffic, but not a lot of profits. Others spend so much money advertising in inappropriate places, primarily due to a lack of tracking responses (learning where the new customers first heard of the business), that they make it impossible to profit, even if their sales rise.

The key and the goal   The key is to home in on your financials so closely that you know the *cost per sale and the profit per sale*. Knowing and lowering that cost per sale is only half the job. Increasing the profit per sale is the goal.

I well remember a meeting that started with a celebratory tone since the sales had been so high and the cost per sale so low. But the meeting ended on a depressing note when it finally came to light that the company was losing money on every sale it made. Up to that point, some of the marketing people were deliriously happy, pointing only to the rising sales curve and high traffic count. They lost sight of their primary goal — profits. And the company suffered a huge loss as a result.

Later the company raised prices, improving its profits, and was able to bring about the glorious relationship between rising sales and rising profits. That's the relationship toward which guerrilla marketing is oriented.

To build consistently healthy profits, you must plan so that you profit on every sale, launch a guerrilla marketing attack and maintain the attack by keeping an eagle eye on the numbers; be impressed only by rising profits.

Without the plan, the numbers may be ugly. Without the consistent marketing attack, they may be pretty, but merely for the short term. Only by succeeding at all three of the tasks listed above can you make marketing work its wonders.

Making marketing work its wonders   There are ten ways guerrillas can increase their profits.

1. Clearly define your company's prime *benefit* to potential customers, along with your *uniqueness*. Consistently present them. These are key reasons that clients or customers patronize a business.
2. Use *direct response* marketing rather than institutional ads. These days, the ask-for-the-order approach is out-pulling the institutional strategy 300 to 1.
3. *Remove all risk* from your customers. How? With an honest 100 percent money-back guarantee and a customer-is-correct policy.

4. *Tell people why* they should do business with your firm. After showing how people will benefit, tell them *why* your firm should be selected rather than another firm.
5. Become a *testing fiend*. Test your offers, letters, postcards, advertisements, headlines, typefaces, and copy. Guerrillas know that testing is crucial for profits. Test the same ad in two papers, which tests the paper. Test different ads in the same paper, which tests the ad. Guerrillas test both.
6. Know the *power of headlines* and feel superior knowing that 90 percent of U.S. companies run ads with no headlines, though headlines can improve response rates up to 2,100 percent.
7. *Test prices*, including *higher prices*. A guerrilla knows that it is not unusual for a $299 price to outpull a $245 price. I've seen a lazy $2.99 cosmetic soar at $6.99.
8. *Increase the length of your copy.* If the information is easy to read and useful, hot prospects will love every word. Guerrillas sell more when they tell more.
9. Make certain *everyone in the organization* is *profit-minded* and sees the relationship between high profits and a glowing future. Offer *profit sharing*.
10. Never lose sight of the fact that *marketing is the engine* that powers every business and profession with profits.

It is not possible to earn profits *all* of the time. Don't expect to fill your coffers to the brim at the very outset when you don't know for certain all of your in-business costs. Don't expect profits during a testing phase. You'll gain data that will result in plenty of profits down the road. But if you manage to break even during testing, you're doing a credible job.

When not to expect profits

Don't look for profits during invest-in-the-future periods when you may have a large capital outlay over a few months and you may just earn profits in excess of that outlay. Worry not. If you've carefully considered your investment, the profits long-term are just as sweet as the profits short-term — and frequently larger.

Don't get the notion that you should profit every day and every month. This is not so. Instead, you should profit more each year than the previous year. Simply by adhering to the fundamentals right here before you, you've got a good head start in the race for financial glee.

Just remember the rule: *profits are the unit of measurement.*

Part Two

Golden Rules to Guide Your Effectiveness

Share of Mind

Guerrilla Marketing's Golden Rule #14:
It is easier to achieve a healthy share of market if you first obtain a healthy share of mind.

MANY COMPANIES AIM for a large share of market. This is a noble effort in that there is nobility in honest profits. But if share of market is your primary aim, you are aiming at a tough-to-hit target.

Your business will obtain that share of market if you aim in a different direction. Guerrilla marketers know that they will gain share of market if they first aim to get share of *mind*. That means prospects not only think of your company, but they think of it *first* when about to purchase what you sell.

You can get that share of mind by your diligent use of the guerrilla marketing weapons and through consistent marketing efforts smack dab to your target audience. You get top-of-the-mind awareness with your commitment to a marketing plan and with your comprehension of the power of *repetition*. **Comprehending the power**

Companies that have gone to the bank by memorizing this concept include Green Giant, Pillsbury, Allstate, Maytag, Starkist, and Kellogg. These weren't always huge corporations. They were once small businesses, too. I single these companies out because their basic marketing themes have run unchanged for 30 to 50 years. They aimed for share of mind and won it. They've even earned a share of your mind. After all, don't you remember the Jolly Green Giant, the Doughboy, the "good hands," the "lonely" repairman, Charlie the Tuna, and Tony the Tiger?

Regardless of the cost or quality of your offering, it is unrealistic to think that one dynamite ad can beautify your bottom line. All it can really do is give you a handhold —

probably not even a firm one — in your prospects' minds. That's not a bad thing; that's good. One little ad followed by others will solidify your handhold, intensify your share of mind.

Solidifying your handhold

If you can provide enough repetition of your product or service name, identity, and overall value, you will eventually secure a healthy share of mind. You can provide such repetition through signs, mailings, phone calls, commercials, print ads, trade show displays, public relations, brochures, and many other weapons of guerrilla marketing, especially through relationships with customers.

Build those relationships with constant attention, with little gifts, previews of new products, services, and prices. You can prove by your actions that the customer means a lot to your business. Ask if there is anything else you can do to make the customer's life a little easier. Listen carefully to the answer, then respond with action.

Where share of mind comes from

Once you've got a healthy share of mind — easy to spot by your increased market share — make special offers and announcements. Watch that market share rise even more. Share of mind comes from publicity, from advertising, from everything you say or do about your business and your customers. Learn the tactics of other guerrillas in your industry by reading trade and marketing publications.

To gain this share of mind, it is crucial that all of your marketing be cohesive. Your letters, signs, ads, comments to customers, packaging — all must shoot for the same goal. Absolute *clarity* is essential to gain a cohesive identity. Be sure all your materials *say the same thing*.

Too many businesses go straight for the jugular, when it is the brain they should be aiming for. Guerrillas with limited budgets know that they need not spend big to get big results. They just have to be sure they are shooting at the right target and that their message is consistent. Plus — they must know the power of repetition. Repetition is the ally of the guerrilla.

Businesses that aim for share of mind are careful not to drop from view for extended periods, or that coveted share of market, for which they also strive, will never be secured. It is simple to understand the importance of gaining a share of mind. But it takes a patient business owner to practice the principles. The wait is well worth it; share of mind is omnipotent in controlling purchase behavior, which becomes share of market for you.

Feel good, however, that it takes even more patience to gain share of market if you don't first claim share of mind. Sometimes business owners never get it at all.

Even a simpleton can see that getting share of market is an uphill hike if a share of mind is not won first. I hope this gives you solace when you run an ad, for example, and fail to break sales records. Realize you have fallen short on that count, but you have increased your share of mind. New sales records will be set in due time.

Nine landmarks reveal the path to success for guerrilla marketers.

A path with nine landmarks

1. The prospect sees your marketing and pays absolutely no attention to it. Don't feel badly. At least he sees it. He misses it two out of every three times you try.
2. Seeing your marketing for a second time is a nonevent for the prospect, who still doesn't really notice you.
3. The prospect realizes he has seen your marketing before somewhere, sometime, and because he's noticed you, he knows you're not another of those fly-by-night operations.
4. The prospect begins to think you're successful. Why? He knows only successful businesses repeat their marketing.
5. Now the prospect decides to find out what you're all about — by reading every word of your copy, perhaps sending away or phoning for more information about your company.
6. By this time you're going nuts because a parade of prospects isn't passing through your front door, but hang in there because the serious prospects are considering a purchase from you.
7. Your hottest prospect actually starts to plan details of the purchase, such as who she must check with first, where

she will get the money, and how she will work the new product into her existing operations.

8. Now the prospect plans the exact date she will visit you, with the express purpose of buying. Maybe she'll call to set an appointment; maybe she'll just drop in some-day soon.

9. The landmark you've been eyeing all along arrives when the purchase takes place — with little sales resistance because the time you have taken for the prospect to no-tice your marketing has earned her trust in you.

These nine landmarks have been identified in a study of how many penetrations of the mind must be accomplished to take a person from total apathy to purchase readiness. It's even more proof of the golden rule that gaining share of market means gaining share of mind first.

Style vs. Substance

Guerrilla Marketing's Golden Rule #15:
Emphasize the meat and potatoes of your offering rather than the plate upon which they're served.

DOES YOUR CURRENT marketing have style or substance? The ideal answer is that your marketing has both. With its style, it conveys your identity and captures the attention of your primary audience. With its substance, your marketing makes essential points and motivates your audience. Guerrillas do their homework and know precisely who wants the benefits of their products or services.

It is apparent that there is room in marketing for both style and substance. But the guerrilla marketer sees to it that both are obvious and that the product or service always has the starring role. If you've ever had the experience of viewing a TV commercial or reading an ad and wondering what the heck they were talking about, you know what I'm getting at. In the early days of advertising nobody needed special effects or computer graphics. When Harley Procter and his cousin James Gamble churned their soap too long and it floated, they came out and said Ivory is the soap that floats. Later, stressing its purity, they said it was 99 and 44/100ths percent pure. People knew exactly what they meant.

99 and 44/100ths percent pure

But now the creative revolution is upon us. In the name of *creativity* rather than the less glamorous but more accurate name of *selling*, hundreds of millions of dollars are being wasted each year. That is a conservative estimate.

The creative rebels, award winners almost every one of them, are carried away by style, and in the melee, substance gets lost. Marketing is not a shuck-and-jive show, a dog-and-pony show, or an entertainment medium. Its purpose is pure selling and it should therefore be loaded with substance.

I'm sad to announce that many of today's professionals have lost sight of that basic fact.

Emphasize the substance

The overriding concept in your marketing should be to *present substance and do it with style.* That means the emphasis is on the substance. The readers and viewers remember the substance. Checks get written, credit cards used, and orders placed because of the substance.

I feel it is my duty to warn you against the multitude of "creative" people that populate the marketing profession. Too many of them have been trained to create a gorgeous picture, a rhyming headline, or a jazzy slogan when they should be trying to create an eye-popping upswing in your sales curve. That sales curve is your responsibility. Remember, if "creative" ideas cost you more than they earn for you, something is wrong with the equation. The equation should read, "creativity equals profits."

Substance consists of both facts and opinions. It communicates both features and benefits. It is as specific as it possibly can be ("99 and 44/100ths percent pure"). And it effectively utilizes both words and pictures. What substance isn't is fun, and you shouldn't try to make people think that it is. That's what style is for. Style is fun. It makes the marketing fun to see and hear.

Hollywood's not the competition

An important point to remember is that your competition isn't Hollywood. It's that company that's been selling to your customers and attracting your prospects. Your competitors are people who don't have stars in their eyes, simply profits on their mind.

Given the relationship of substance to style, and the reasons that you should put your money on substance every time — you should nonetheless be aware of the exceptions to this golden rule.

If, for example, the very essence of a product or service is its style, you may want to convey that style as its primary benefit to its target market. The style *is* the substance.

The marketing of cosmetics, designer clothes, automobiles,

cigarettes, and beer often successfully employs style over substance. Whereas some companies feature the product itself in
their marketing, others focus on ecology, second mortgages,
safe sex — topics that have nothing to do with their products,
but a lot to do with their target markets.

Frequently the mood or atmosphere of the marketing —
whether it be enigmatic, provocative, or radical — is critical.
It enables the members of the target market to identify with
the brand being marketed. The purpose of this marketing
technique is still to sell the product. But the purpose is accomplished by projecting images, impressions, and illusions, by
reflecting the attitudes of the target market.

Is this style or is it substance? It is pure substance — but
once again, the substance is style. In many cases, the guerrillas know that associating their offering with the values of their
prospects is the surest way to a sale.

**Style may be
the substance**

Marketing never was considered a means of social responsibility, but the 1990s saw the birth of marketing that at-
tempted to sell goods while saving the planet. This is known
as the era of "green" rather than the era of "greed" that characterized the 1980s. Enlightened companies are portraying
themselves as individuals with souls rather than faceless corporate entities.

However, the exceptions to the rule of substance over style
are few. Most people should not even *think* of selling with
style at the expense of substance. Many have tried. Most have
failed.

The golden rule is stress your substance, but do it with
style.

Being Interesting

Guerrilla Marketing's Golden Rule #16:
Your marketing has an obligation to capture the attention and hold the interest of as many prospects as possible.

REGARDLESS OF the content of your marketing, the glory of your prose, the timeless beauty of your graphics, and the energetic dedication of your sales force, it is all meaningless to people who have paid no attention to it.

Guerrillas don't let that happen. Their marketing flags the attention of their prospects. This is not easy to do. Most marketing either gains no attention at all or draws attention to the wrong element of the marketing. You must not only gain the attention of likely purchasers, which is difficult enough, but you must also hold on to that attention until it motivates the prospects to purchase — and long after, too.

The media abounds with well-planned advertisements that fail because the planning did not include the gaining of attention. If you're to sell what you sell, you've certainly got to **The first step** interest your prospects. And the first step in gaining *interest* is gaining *attention*.

Be sure you gain it with something very pertinent to your product or service. Ideally, your product or service will gain attention for you because of the benefits it offers.

As every guerrilla knows, you've got to be fine-tuned to your customers and prospects. This way, you can take a firm grasp on the attention you have attracted and direct it toward your offering, clearly showing how it can improve the prospect's life. Because you can talk about things from your prospect's point of view, you can generate a high level of interest. If you don't know your market intimately, you can't be intimate with your market. Result: fewer sales.

Being able to say "This solar heating system can save you $188 per month based upon your current use of energy" is more interesting than saying "Over one thousand photovoltaic cells turn light into electricity in this unit." Both are fascinating, to be sure. But the first one hits home.

Always remember that people do not read print ads, do not read brochures, do not read Yellow Pages ads, do not read direct mail letters, do not listen to telemarketing pitches, do not listen to radio commercials, do not watch TV commercials, and do not pay attention to fancy company video brochures.

What people do not read

Instead, they read only what interests them, listen to only what interests them, view only what interests them. The meaning: you've got to do everything in your power to interest them. Not just with your headline and copy, but all the way until the purchase.

What are people interested in?

1. Themselves
2. How your offering benefits them
3. The importance of those benefits
4. Not being ripped off
5. Why they should buy right now

Your job is simply to tell them what they are interested in. If you've got a complex or technical story — the two do not necessarily go hand-in-hand — tell it in their terms and show how it helps them. Tell the fascinating facts about your product, but only as it relates to your prospects. Reassure them with guarantees and testimonials that they will not be ripped off. Give them a powerful reason to buy right now and not "think it over." That really means "put it off." The guerrilla knows that a purchase *will* be made and does everything possible to be the one who makes the sale.

There are ten other techniques that you can use to capture attention and maintain interest.

Ten techniques to maintain interest

1. Know that headlines are the name of the game in ads. If you're going to perfect your ad, concentrate on perfecting your headline.

2. Although trillions of people may read your words, direct your language to one person at a time. Keep the tone personal rather than "mass market."

3. Use words that have an announcement quality, that promise something new, that feel newsy.

4. Talk about how easy it is to afford your offering, stressing the easy payments, the long-term economy, the reduced price, or the classic nature of it.

5. Give valuable advice that can help your prospect, proving your expertise.

6. Include testimonials — not entire letters, but quotes from satisfied people. The more your prospect can relate to the people quoted, the better for you.

7. Be as specific as possible. Remove the adjectives and be generous with names and numbers.

8. Address your message to an intelligent person, because that's who will read your message. Don't talk over anyone's head or beneath their dignity.

9. Use short paragraphs, short sentences, short words. Your overall message need not be short, but these components of your message should be.

10. Use visuals to augment your words. Visuals can take the form of photos — generally considered more effective than illustrations — illustrations (if you must), diagrams, charts, and graphs. Expect high readership of the captions.

Hurry up and say it Never lose sight of the fact that the reader has a limited time schedule, so cut down on the number of words you use. Each is precious.

One common error is the interesting opening followed by sheer boredom. Work hard to keep every word interesting so the reader always wants more.

Many people who create marketing, especially those who pay for it, want it to be directed to everyone and to interest everyone. This is hardly ever possible. Instead, your job is to focus the message and limit the market. Rather than saying everything to no one, you'll end up saying something to someone. And that's a worthy goal.

Because you've studied that someone, you know what he is interested in, and you know the benefits that push his hot buttons. Throughout your marketing, maintain the interest of all the someones on your customer and prospect lists, and you'll see how *interest* translates itself into *income*.

Timing

SOMETIMES A COMPANY actively markets a wonderful product or service to the appropriate target audience in superbly selected media. But the marketing turns out to be a flop because of poor timing.

A ski bus announces its service during a year with no snow. A real estate firm produces a color brochure during a severely depressed year for real estate. Good ideas. Terrible timing. So long, good ideas.

All time is not created equal All time is not created equal. In order to get the most mileage from your marketing, you've got to be keenly attuned to the right times and the wrong times. Some times are far more propitious to your success than other times. Guerrillas know the difference. If they didn't, they wouldn't be guerrillas.

To gain a bit of insight, consider these ten examples:

1. You've created the perfect mailing package, but it arrives too early in the week, when your prospect is thinking of the week ahead, or too late, when your prospect is thinking of the upcoming weekend. Moral: depending upon what you are selling, determine when your mailer should arrive, then arrange for it to arrive on that exact day.

2. You've got a fine product but a limited budget and a lot of competition. What to do? Do your marketing when your competitors have eased up and you can gain the largest share of mind with the smallest marketing investment. Maybe that will be during what are deemed the slow months. But it's when you can attract the most attention the fastest.

3. Everybody receives Christmas catalogues in September

and October. If you sent yours during June or July, you'd get people thinking of your company then and later on as well. It's a bit crazy, but if you explain why you are mailing at that time, it will make sense to your prospects. Naturally, this approach can be applied to any holiday season.

4. Keep abreast of current events by watching the tube, reading newspapers, perusing newsweeklies, and subscribing to publications within your industry. Then tie in your offerings with what is happening at that moment in history. A depression is ugly except to businesspeople who realize it is an ideal opportunity for them to make sales. During every depression some companies prosper, some entrepreneurs are transformed into millionaires.

5. Be careful not to launch your marketing too soon. One of the most common errors is to market before all the bugs have been worked out, before the salespeople know all the facts, before you are ready to fill the flood of orders. Remember, patience is a guerrilla virtue. Marketing before the product is available is both suicidal and silly.

6. Some of the saddest events in marketing are the snazzy newspaper story or the bigtime TV report about products that are not yet in distribution. The business owner is so enthralled at the thought of free publicity that the news is released before people can buy the product. The people won't come back another time and the media won't give you another splash. Restraint is necessary even with free news coverage. Don't be tempted to grant that interview to the reporter — because if the story runs and people flock to the stores to purchase your product and it isn't in stock, the intelligent retailer will switch that customer to a different product and you may have lost her for life. With millions of potential customers lost, you'll be doomed before you get going. And you could have prevented this business disaster simply by asking the reporter to wait, then getting back to him at a later date. How many times have I seen a company bury itself with premature publicity? Too many times, and it's most avoidable.

A sad moment

7. Savvy retailers wait a month before having their grand openings. If they don't, customers will come flocking in to find

untrained salespeople, poorly stocked shelves, slow delivery times, clumsy sales procedures, and messy surroundings. Polish these items to perfection before your grand opening — or it won't be so grand. Is it actually possible to permanently turn people off during a grand opening? Only when the sun rises in the East.

8. Telemarketing calls that don't get through or that reach answering devices are a waste of time and money. Find out when your prospects are most likely to be at the phone, and then do your telemarketing. It may be at 11:00 A.M. for businesses and at 6:30 P.M. for home owners. The first goal of a phone call is to reach the prospect.

9. Deal quickly with customer requests, orders, and complaints. People revere their time these days more than ever. Revere it with them. If they have to wait one hour longer than they expected, years of your planning may go down the tubes because of your tardiness. It's better to tell a customer there's a three-week wait and then deliver in three weeks than to tell her there's a one-week wait, then deliver in two weeks. Asking them to wait isn't nearly as bad as wasting their time or misleading them on matters concerning their time.

Years of planning down the tubes

10. Never create your marketing materials in a rush. While they are being developed, you can aim for quality, economy, or speed — choose any two, but not all three. The guerrilla chooses quality and economy.

The management of a small company that makes patio furniture wanted to introduce their new line in the summertime, but they knew they would be outspent by competitors. Solution? They introduced their new line during the winter when the competitors were not actively marketing. Result? Short- and long-term success.

An inventory of marketing materials

Many companies maintain an *inventory of marketing materials*. Rather than creating the materials when they need them, the usual way of doing things, these far-sighted companies have a prepared selection of direct mail letters, radio commercials, brochures, print ads, and other weapons of guerrilla marketing.

The materials wait in the wings until the time is right to

use them. The newspaper announces an upcoming heat wave. The guerrilla company runs its hot-weather ad. The home team wins the championship. The guerrilla company runs its congratulations ad. The TV news show announces impending inflation. The guerrilla company runs its preinflation commercials. Prepared for any eventuality, these companies time their marketing to the news of the moment. If they'd had to start from scratch to prepare these materials, the news would have been long forgotten by the time the materials were ready.

The key to timing properly is being ready with just the right weapon. Guerrilla companies capitalize on opportunities others miss because they plan for them in advance and are ready to roll at a moment's notice. Perfect timing is the result of perfect planning. This golden rule tells you never to leave things up to fate.

Cleverness

Guerrilla Marketing's Golden Rule #18:
People will remember the most clever part of your marketing; be sure it pertains directly to what you are selling.

A BUSINESS WILL often bleed attention away from its primary benefit — even from its name — just because the owner thinks marketing is supposed to be clever. Marketing must be many things, but *clever* is not among them.

There is no evidence that headlines are supposed to rhyme or make puns. There are no case histories of companies that soared to glory on the wings of cleverness alone. Be sure you aim constantly to make your product or service the *only* thing that is clever in your marketing.

Unless used with surgical precision, cleverness gets in the way of sound marketing, but many creators of marketing find **Easy to be clever** it easier to be clever than to be motivating. The idea is to create a desire to buy, not to amuse readers and viewers.

If you must be clever, be sure that your product or service is what's really being clever, not some outside entity. At one time or another, everyone has heard someone describe "this amazing commercial I saw last night." "Who was the commercial for?" you ask. "I can't remember," comes the answer, "but it sure was a clever commercial."

Don't ever let this happen to your marketing. I think of the products I have purchased in my lifetime, and although I can recall a few that came to my attention because of their marketing, I can't think of any that won me over by being clever.

Because people will remember your most clever line or **The star** graphic, *be sure that the star is your offering* or you're sunk. Being deep-sixed by your own marketing is not clever at all.

Many advertisements have garnered millions of chuckles and a host of awards while the product lost a fortune.

If you want to entertain people, go into show business. That is definitely not the purpose of marketing. Guerrillas have a radar against cleverness. Red lights flash and loud bells ring in their brains when they see a rhyming headline or a cute little pun that gets smack dab in the way of their most important selling point.

This is not to say that cleverness has no place in marketing, but unless the cleverness is used *to advance the sale*, be wary of it. It could do more damage than good.

Knowing this all to be true, I am astonished at the millions spent daily on witty, pretty marketing that is totally ineffective. If marketing is not supposed to be clever, then just what should it be?

If not clever, then what?

1. It should be surprising in its message.
2. It should be clear about the prime benefit.
3. It should involve the reader or viewer.
4. It should challenge curiosity.
5. It should command action.
6. It should let readers think.
7. It should be one unit: words and pictures.
8. It should be devoid of braggadocio.
9. It should be well-executed and credible.
10. It should motivate enough to lead to a sale.

Notice how none of these ten properties of great marketing involve being clever or beautiful. The beauty in great marketing can be found in your bottom line. The genius in creating it involves making the plain truth fascinating. The plain truth is about how your product or service can benefit or solve the problems of your target audience. If you must be clever about anything, be clever about *that*.

If you make a concerted effort to focus on the benefits you offer, you will probably end up with wise marketing. This effort will force you either to be clever about your product's benefits or to abandon cleverness altogether.

I assume that you, as a reader of a book on marketing, have a lot of money — or at least some money — dependent upon the success or failure of marketing. If this is true, and it is your own money or your stockholders' money, you'll avoid cleverness like the plague.

But if you are a writer, artist, or producer with none of your own money tied up in the effectiveness of marketing, you won't feel the crying need to stay the heck away from cleverness. If you're part *artiste*, as too many professional marketing creators are, you'll be tempted to create the marketing materials that will win awards, compliments from your peer group, and maybe even plaudits from an adoring public.

Avoid the temptation But the way the world works, that public buys products and services, not clever marketing lines. Avoid the temptation to be clever just for the sake of cleverness.

The guerrilla uses cleverness only *when it is necessary to make a point*, such as the Energizer Bunny making the point of the long-lasting power of Energizer batteries. Such ideas are rare, and coming close doesn't count. Unless you score a bull's-eye, you probably have wasted a marketing investment.

The guerrilla avoids cleverness, avoids anything that will be more interesting than his or her product or service, avoids drawing attention away from the main benefit.

Recognize that great marketing can be startling, amazing, and riveting. When it is, the greatness comes from the product or service being startling, amazing, and riveting. A lack of cleverness does not mean a lack of interest. Marketing can be superb in every way without being clever.

A heartless thief Think of cleverness as a heartless thief, robbing your message of its power and robbing you of your marketing investment. The purpose of your marketing must be to create a powerful desire to buy what you are selling — not to entertain, amuse, and win meaningless accolades.

Because cleverness is so endemic among failed marketing attempts, this golden rule obviously guides too few people.

Bribes

Guerrilla Marketing's Golden Rule #19:
Whatever term you use to describe it, the truth remains that everybody loves a bribe.

I HOPE YOU DON'T think this rule advises you to slip somebody a wad of money under the table in order to procure an order. That is not ethical conduct, and guerrilla marketing shuns any breach of ethics.

Instead, when a guerrilla refers to a bribe, the guerrilla means a gift given to a prospect or customer to encourage a response to a marketing offer or to intensify a relationship. The polite, and more commonly used, term for bribes is *advertising specialities*. Unlike premiums which may require a purchase, bribes are given for free and offered for free in marketing. They work on all demographic groups, from paupers to millionaires. Most companies use bribes to generate leads, increase name awareness, make friends, thank customers, introduce new things, and motivate people to act.

Even millionaires love 'em

As of late 1990, the most popular bribes in the U.S. were T-shirts and caps, writing instruments, desk and office accessories, and glassware and ceramics. Matchbooks, while on the decline, still pulled in 800,000 responses for International Correspondence Schools in 1988. That's hot stuff. Marketing people invest over $14 billion in bribes each year. The reasons: they fit almost any ad budget; they complement other media; they can be directed to selected audiences; people jump through hoops to get them for free. About the only disadvantage is the teensy space available to say anything to the recipient. There's no place for long copy.

No long copy

So do they work? Well, 40 percent of people who receive free gifts can remember the name of the advertiser as long as six months later. And 31 percent use the gift at least one year after receiving it. That's not even counting the high response rate.

Probably the most popular of the old-time bribes were calendars. Today, with the average household having four calendars, you'd be smart to consider them again.

A recent study proved that bribes not only increase mail response, but also raise the dollar purchase per sale a whopping 321 percent. Don't limit your thinking on ad specialties to the mail. They're very effective for guerrillas at trade-show booths, open houses, special events, and grand openings. They generate positive feelings and an unconscious sense of obligation — to buy from you.

Six questions   Once you've made the decision to try a bribe, ask these six questions:

1. How many people do I want to reach?
2. How much money do I have to spend?
3. What message do I want to print?
4. What gift will be most useful to my prospects?
5. Is this unique and desirable?
6. Is the gift matched to my target audience?

Then contact one of the 12,000 manufacturing and distributing firms or one of the 4,000 members of the Specialty Advertising Association International and ask to look through their colorful and copious catalogues. You'll probably be pleased at both the selection and the prices.

Companies that use enticements say that during the period of bribing, their marketing should focus on the bribe to maximize the response they get from their offer. The high response rate to a company's showing a color photo of the enticement while offering it for free boggles the mind. This pow-
Sleazy but   erful method increases responses, leads, and profits. Bribes are
powerful   known to be addictive to the companies that offer them. The addiction is to the results.

Sure, there will always be the curiosity seekers and freebie seekers who will respond to your offering. But you won't mind them when you see the dazzling potency that a free gift brings to your business. A client of mine now sends out postcards with color photos of the bribe being offered and the words "A free gift for you!" Response rates are staggering. And yet there's not a word about the benefits of doing business with the company!

At first glance, this appears to be ineffective marketing. But the high response rates and profit-per-response prove that it is, although unusual, extremely effective marketing. Just remember to follow up your offer with a sales call, brochure, or some other means which will tell the customer the value of doing business with you.

The company with the "free gift for you!" approach rode to glory on the power of bribes, using them to motivate prospects to request further information. Lackluster marketing became a high-profit investment when bribes were added to the marketing mix.

There are many excellent catalogues of free gifts; I suggest you call a local company selected from your Yellow Pages, and ask to see their catalogue. Talk about your goals with their representative. The time spent with the advertising specialty rep will not only get your feet wet when it comes to the ways a great bribe can be targeted to a wide variety of audiences, but will also show you the surprisingly low costs for items with high perceived values.

If you're going to offer bribes, be sure they not only have the *perceived value*, but also the *quality* that people want. A free quartz desk clock that looks like a million bucks, costs you less than two bucks, and breaks the first week your prospect uses it, isn't going to win any friends or sales for you. Your intentions may have been noble, but your taste in advertising specialties left much to be desired. When guerrillas follow a golden rule, they follow it properly and not haphazardly.

One of the most winning aspects of a bribe is its ability to allow you to use the word "free" honestly, liberally, and proudly. Show me someone who doesn't like a free gift and I'll show you an extraterrestrial alien. When we get our space program advanced far enough, we'll probably find that even the critters from beyond our solar system light up at the thought of a valuable present at absolutely no cost. For marketing to

Momentum   move from a standing start to a completed sale, momentum is required. Offers of free gifts start that momentum.

Whatever you do, don't give away a bribe until you have defined exactly what you want it to accomplish. If you don't have a clearly stated goal for the bribe, avoid offering it. You shouldn't waste the money — even though some bribes are in the less-than-a-cent range.

What, then, might be the goals of a bribe? Here are ten:

1. To get a person to send for your brochure
2. To get a person to request a sales call
3. To reward a person for being a new or repeat customer
4. To serve as an incentive for specific behavior
5. To reward results among a sales staff
6. To get people to complete a survey
7. To motivate people to make a purchase
8. To motivate people to enlarge the size of their purchase
9. To increase morale, sales, safety, attendance, and more
10. To make your name a brand name

As important as the *planning* of a bribe promotion are the *analysis and evaluation* of the program. Guerrillas use bribes at every opportunity to profit from this golden rule.

Economizing

Guerrilla Marketing's Golden Rule #20:
The key to marketing economically is not in saving money, but in making every investment pay off handsomely.

WHEN MOST PEOPLE think about marketing, they think about spending money. Nothing wrong with that mindset. After all, the guerrilla knows that marketing is not really an expense if you do it right; it's an investment.

Some people think they can save money by ceasing marketing. That's a bad idea. Thinking that stopping your marketing can save money is a lot like thinking that stopping your watch can save time. Life doesn't work that way.

If you want the best of both worlds — aggressive marketing plus saving money — I suggest you try some or all of these fourteen ideas:

Fourteen ways to save

1. Realize that small is beautiful. Instead of using a big ad agency, consider working with a consultant or a free-lancer. Realize that many small ads are better than just a few large ads. Run 30-second spots instead of 60-second spots. See if you can make your point in 15 seconds. The majority of TV spots in the U.S. are now under 30 seconds.

2. Place your ads through your own house agency or through a media-buying service. You save money with the former, 15 percent of your ad cost; you save both time *and* money with the latter. And you get professional consultation thrown in.

3. Obtain free research by relying on industry publications, reference librarians, and by creating your own customer questionnaire. Study the answers to the questions to gain clues about your customers' minds; study the handwriting on the questions for clues about customer personality types.

4. Look into regional editions of national magazines. Consider buying remnant magazine space at even lower cost. Call Media Networks, Inc. at 1-800-225-3457 and request their free media kit; you'll be astonished at the low price for advertising in high-prestige magazines.

5. Experiment and test your marketing. That way, you'll be able to run only proven successes, not shots in the dark. Failure to experiment is a common and expensive mistake. Remember that guerrillas are patient and willing to experiment before committing. The simplest tests measure one thing at a time: price, headline, offer, medium, layout, target audience. Experiment with small publications, small markets, small mailing lists. Expect to break even during experimentation, but to learn a billion bucks worth of information.

You'd rather fight than switch

6. Stick with one marketing campaign. Don't switch around. This will not only lower your production costs, it will also increase the effectiveness of your marketing. Failure to adhere to this point is the reason for the greatest waste of marketing funds in America, and it always has been.

7. Write timeless ads and brochures. Don't say "Our company is five years old." Next year that will have to be updated. Instead, say "Our company was founded in 1988." And don't show photos of employees in your marketing. Next month one of them might get busted for selling crack. Judge your brochures through the eyes of a customer in the future as well as the present. Creating a new brochure every year is decidedly unguerrillalike behavior.

8. Find multiple uses for your marketing materials. Blow up a panel of your brochure to use as an ad. Make it larger and use it as a poster or a sign. Don't worry about paying, say, $1,000 for a photograph. If you can use it in ten applications for ten years, your real cost is $10 per use of a dynamite photo. A tiny investment, and a wise one.

9. Gain access to co-op advertising funds, marketing money often made available to small businesses by large manufacturers. In 1990, nearly $3 billion in co-op funds went unclaimed. If you deal with a manufacturer, ask about their co-op program. If they don't have one, ask that they establish

one. Some guerrillas have half their marketing budget covered by co-op monies. In such arrangements, you mention the manufacturer and possibly show its logo and say its theme line. For doing so, you are given a percentage of the ad or commercial cost. Everyone profits.

10. Look into P.O. arrangements with the media. P.O. stands for "per order" — meaning that the medium gets a percentage of each sale you make. This gives you the media at no upfront cost, eliminating your risk and transferring it to the media. If they think they'll turn a handsome profit, they'll enter into this arrangement as they have with hundreds of other firms. All you've got to do is ask.

11. If you'll be printing something in color, be willing to wait and get in on a gang run. You wait longer; you save money. Gang runs are when the printer runs a large color press run. Your color might be a wee bit off and you might not obtain immediate service, but you can save big, big money.

12. Reprint any publicity stories about you or your company and use them in your mailings, as signs, in brochures, in press kits, as framed display pieces, and as sales aids for your reps. Yesterday's newspaper is dead and gone; yesterday's PR story can — and should — live forever.

13. If you're about to do a direct mailing, try to do it with a postcard if possible. You can save money and increase your response rate at the same time. Make it a color postcard and you'll get the best of both worlds. Color increases readership by 41 percent and raises a buyer's inclination to buy by 26 percent. The cost? Lower than you think. Call Adcolor, a low-cost, high-quality printer, at 1-800-232-1544 to see the low cost and high quality yourself.

Colorful increases

14. Recognize that although in 1990 the *average* TV commercial cost $193,000 to produce, many superb TV spots were shot for under $1,000. A lot of these worked better than the costly ones. Effectiveness comes from ideas, not production values.

The two biggest mistakes in marketing are spending too little and spending too much. Guerrillas make neither mistake.

The two biggest mistakes

If you're bound and determined to save money, then spend your time and energy saving money by marketing to your current customers rather than drumming up new ones. Guerrillas know that it costs five times as much to sell to a new customer as to an existing one.

Save even more money by actively pursuing fusion marketing arrangements where you help a few companies market by distributing their brochures or putting up their signs in return for them doing the same for you. This not only economizes for you, but also markets to more people.

Look into reaching your market through classified ads; more publications than ever offer them. Say one great thing about your firm, then ask people to call or write for your free brochure. Costs get smaller while your prospect list gets larger. Gain classified data from Classified Communication, a company specializing in classified ads, by calling 602-778-6788.

The most practical, obvious, and sensible method of economizing is one practiced by a *minority* of business owners but by *all* guerrilla business owners: operate from a marketing plan and calendar. Your greatest economy will come from your third year's marketing calendar. You learn the first year, improve the second year, perfect the third year, and benefit from this golden rule forever after.

Soft Steps and Hard Steps

Guerrilla Marketing's Golden Rule #21:
It is easier to get someone to take the hard step of buying if they first take the softer step of requesting more data.

BUSINESS WOULD BE a breeze and guerrillas could devote their talents elsewhere if customers walked right in and handed over their money.

But we know that business doesn't even pretend to be a breeze, and we know that guerrillas have got to give their company all they've got before any customer walks in and hands anyone any money.

It sounds tough and it is tough, but don't think you've got it tough until you've looked at the idea of buying something through the eyes of a customer. That's who really has it tough. **The poor** The customer can waste money, time, make a dumb mistake, **customer** be ridiculed by friends, even be fired for making such a stupid purchase.

Handing that money over to you — in the form of a check, credit card, cash, purchase order, or barter agreement — is a hard step to take. It is one not taken lightly. And in many cases, it is one not taken at all. Don't forget, there are scads of other businesses out there vying for the customer's money. Some are your direct competitors. Some are indirect competitors. For example, the travel and leisure business works hard to convince you that it's a trip to Mexico that you really want, while the electronics industry is making a strong case for your buying a new giant-screen TV or a digital tape recorder. These businesses, and many more, want your customer's money. Few customers can give their money to everyone, so they have to be highly selective.

The guerrilla doesn't just sit there during that all-important selection process. *The guerrilla becomes involved in it.* Guerrillas make it easy as pie to take the hard step of buying from them. They accomplish that by offering soft steps that can be taken prior to the hard step. They help customers make their selection.

Make it easy to say yes

A soft step softens up a customer, asking very little, making it easy to proceed, simple to say yes. A hard step asks a lot from the customer. But it's easier for them to say yes if they've been softened up.

You can soften them up with information, with service, and with your caring attitude. A list of soft steps is coming up in just a moment. All of those steps make it extremely easy to take that hard step — in fact, it doesn't even seem hard anymore because prospects have been working their way toward it, guided by you, step by step, with your sensitive marketing.

In every sales situation there's a hard step. In most sales situations there are also several soft steps, or at least one. There is no evidence that the quantity of soft steps affects profitability, but ample data supports the premise that quality soft steps can increase profits.

The underlying force

Every guerrilla knows that before a sale is made, momentum must be created. One of the most valuable ways to create momentum is to get customers to say yes. This is the underlying force behind soft steps.

Do you want our free video brochure? Yes.

Do you want a free sample? Yes.

Are you looking for a 24-hour-a-day plumber? (Asked of a truly hot and wet prospect who is frantically checking the Yellow Pages at 3:00 A.M.) Yes!

Ten soft steps

Although prospects do not readily say yes to the hard step, they will frequently say it to the soft steps. This is why soft steps were created. Just what are the soft steps exactly? They are different from bribes because they are far more than a free gift; they are a direct introduction to your products or services. They are weapons that create the momentum that leads to the hard step. Here are ten to give you some clues:

1. An offer of a free videotape
2. An offer of a free audiotape
3. An offer of a free brochure
4. An offer of a free sample
5. An offer of a free demonstration
6. An offer of a free consultation
7. An offer of a free booklet
8. An offer of a free estimate
9. An offer to attend a free seminar
10. An offer of a free newsletter

Have I left out any soft steps? You bet! Every time you run an ad you are taking a soft step, softening up the customer, and moving a wee bit closer to that hard step. Perhaps you are even asking questions in your ads and commercials, conditioning customers to get in the habit of saying yes to your offers.

To succeed in guerrilla marketing, concentrate on generating the momentum that leads to a sale. Think of the soft steps you can take. Make a list of them, then have a brainstorming session with your coworkers to see any others they can dream up. It is better to have too many soft steps than too few. Are you making it easy to say yes? Let that answer light your way.

Each soft step must have the intent and capability of leading directly to the hard step. Although you and I know that they are merely steps on the way to a goal, they should be totally self-sufficient and capable of generating a completed sale all by themselves. Each soft step should try to get your prospect to sign up right then and there.

The best soft steps I've seen combine awareness gained through *media exposure* with an offer of a *free brochure* and a *free consultation*. That's three soft steps and it's usually **Three may be** enough. Just ten years ago one step, the hard step, may have **enough** been enough. But when you're in the middle of an information age, you've just got to be prepared to offer information to people who justifiably ask for it. And three steps seems the right number for most companies.

Step one gets your company past the "stranger" barrier.

Step two provides your prospect with information. Step three puts everything on a personalized basis. You can see why the hard step is relatively simple after three soft steps. The soft steps answered questions, defused anxieties, established a relationship, and set the stage for a yes.

The best guerrillas are patient people who are willing and able to follow the golden rule of soft steps right to the dotted line.

One-on-One: Micro-Marketing

Guerrilla Marketing's Golden Rule #22:
Tiny shares of gigantic markets are abundant and profitable if you serve and market to one person at a time.

YOU NEED NOT be a dominant force to be a successful capitalist. You can be a teeny tiny multimillionaire by mastering the guerrilla's ability of pinpointing your prime prospects and understanding the real meaning of *prime*.

To a guerrilla, *prime prospects* is more than a phrase: it's an art form. To some guerrilla business owners, prime prospects are the people most likely to make the purchase *right at this very instant*.

If you had to zero in on the most prime of your prospects, these would be the cream. It is very important for you to locate these people because of one hot fact: *They are looking for someone like you and they want to buy what you're selling.*

It's easy to serve and market to these people because simply by stating a fact, your offer can help them single themselves out as ready to buy. For example, a headline that starts with "If you're in the market to buy a bed . . ." is clearly going to be read by your prime prospects — if you sell beds.

But *prime* refers to another category of prospects as well: huge companies. These prospects are so worthwhile to you as potential customers that they deserve the time and energy it takes to go one-on-one with them.

When you go one-on-one, you market not by selling, but by helping. Guerrillas call this consultive selling because they **Consultive selling** serve as much as a counselor and adviser as a salesperson. They have such a sincere and heartfelt desire to help their customers that they establish the relationship before they make the sale. If you do this properly, you pave the way to your sale.

Guerrillas who market with consultive selling are not in a hurry, expect no instant results, and have exercised so much selectivity in the prospects they help that it is almost always worth their wait. That's how rich the payoff will be. A small company marketed to a huge corporation for two years, providing information and services at no cost. When the corporation finally bought from the small company, its order was large enough to generate a full year's healthy profits by itself. Even if the small firm earned profits from no other customer, it earned enough from this one to have a dazzling year on its bottom line. Consultive selling and two-year waits are not for all companies. But if yours is one that can benefit, look into it because consultive selling is a portent of a profitable future.

Many one-on-ones   Naturally, because this company was doing its one-on-one marketing with more than just one company, its profits multiplied even more. Yet it had few customers. A small customer list does not mean small bank deposits. A firm I know of had a less than a one-tenth of one percent share of its market, hardly dominating, but many of its employees were earning fortunes.

Friends in low places   If I were you, I'd wonder how a guerrilla markets to a huge corporation. The answer is *by having friends in low places*.

You don't market to the president or marketing director. Instead you market to the people *who will use* your products or services. These will probably be department heads or production foremen. Guerrillas often wear Levi's as part of their uniform. They are attired in quality offerings.

The route to success with micro-marketing, as every guerrilla reader knows, is provided to you through *information*. Note that I did not say money; I said information. It does not cost a lot to micro-market. It does take a lot of brainwork and legwork. It takes a persistently caring attitude. It takes technology in the form of computer expertise and software that helps you zero in on your market. An ultimate example of this technology is being able, thanks to your computer and databanks, to select the 50 hottest prospects for your firm from a list of 50,000. Fed the right data, the computer can do the job.

The keys to becoming a techno-guerrilla are to train your staff and then train them some more. Don't expect them to take to computers quickly. If you won't train, stay low-tech. If you stay low-tech, reconsider micro-marketing.

Because you need as much information as possible, especially to help you focus on the cream of the prospects and to provide as much help to them as possible, computers are nearly mandatory for one-on-one marketing. If you're going to market to one person at a time, as this golden rule says you must do, you must be sure you're directing your energies at the right person. The five steps in micro-marketing are

1. *Identify your prime prospects.* This task requires great discrimination on your part.
2. *Create marketing materials to help your prospects,* all in the form of useful information.
3. *Secure an appointment with the right person* at the right company, after determining who that person is and how he or she will benefit from your offering.
4. *Establish rapport with that person,* a level of trust that gives you credibility, and one that is earned by active listening on your part.
5. *Provide constant attention and help for your customer* to prevent apathy and lost customers while helping your current customers grow. Customer growth is the guerrilla's most fulfilling source of profits.

The underlying strategy of one-on-one marketing is exactly the opposite of traditional marketing. Your goals are

- A small, select customer list
- Trusting relationships
- New information to help your prospect
- Sales generated through service
- Giving unexpected values

It is fairly simple to follow this golden rule if you are not greedy and are able to pinpoint the people who can help your company the most in the long run.

The Danger of Originality

Guerrilla Marketing's Golden Rule #23:
Don't invest money in originality when the investment
should be in generating profits.

ORIGINALITY. It's what collectors look for in fine art. It's what entrepreneurs avoid in guerrilla marketing.

Watch out for originality. Be on guard for its presence. Look askance at it. Suspect anything that hints of it. More marketing dollars have been wasted in the senseless quest for originality than in the noble quest for profits.

If there's anything *not* to be as a guerrilla, it's original.

The whole idea is to develop your marketing plan, create your marketing materials — then run with them — again and again and again. Run them until they stop working. Most people quit running them before they have a chance to start working. They get tired of the "same old thing" (though it's never the "same old thing" to customers and prospects) and they want something different, something original.

A red flag is waving

Danger flag! Be warned away from originality by that red flag waving in your face. "Tried and true" doesn't sound as much fun as "highly original." But it's the route to follow if you're to be a guerrilla. Get your fun by putting money in the bank, not into original marketing.

I met with my new client and we reviewed the marketing in which he had engaged last year. He pointed out that the promotion he used in March was the *single most successful promotion* in the history of his six-year-old business. But the marketing he used the other eleven months was a relative bust and didn't come near producing the record-breaking numbers he enjoyed with his March promotion.

"Why didn't you repeat the promotion you used in March?" I asked. "Say, that's a good idea!" said the client. "Why, *I never thought of that.*" **Astonishing but true**

With another client, I reviewed the ads he had been running over the past five years. He knew which ones were incredibly profitable and which were miserably wasteful. "Why didn't you continue running the ads that pulled so well for you?" I inquired. "Hmmm, *you think that would work out for me, right?*" asked the client.

Still another meeting comes to mind. This one was with a sophisticated client who was in a deep quandary. His marketing was working wonders, but he had a nagging suspicion that he should change it. When I asked why, he had no answer — just this vague notion that marketing should be changed, that even successful marketing should be replaced with original marketing.

The opposite of all this nonsense was the client who broke the bank with a specific promotion. "Any reason I can't repeat it next month?" he inquired. "Nope," I replied sagely, knowing the deck was stacked in his favor. "Do it again. And even again if it works the second time."

Two months later he called to report that sales continued to rise and asked if he could run the same promotion just one more time. "Why only one more time?" I asked. "Stay with it until it stops working."

To his surprise, it *never stopped working.* Until he sold his business for a sinfully high profit several years later, he used that same promotion *six times a year.*

I spoke with a client who talked of an ad her company ran a decade ago. "Every time it ran," she told me, "it more than paid for itself. Do you think we should run the same ad now?" This is what I call an easy question. It required little guerrilla genius for me to counsel her to stay the course. **An easy question**

I love new movies. My wife creates original collages and art constructions. We enjoy theatrical debuts. But I wouldn't dream of experimenting with originality using my client's money in the arena of marketing. Although novelty is a boon to certain industries, it is generally toxic to marketing.

Brochures, ads, TV spots, radio commercials, and direct marketing pieces that are original — never before seen by the prospects — might draw attention to their originality and away from the prime offer, might confuse the prospects by virtue of their originality, and might arouse within the prospect a deep appreciation of art rather than a deep desire to buy.

Originality is not worth this risk to you. Too much is known about marketing for you to explore new and dangerous terrain. I well realize that *some* marketing is both motivating and original. I also know that even a broken wristwatch gives the correct time twice a day.

If you start out trying to be original, something is going to get lost along the way — the strategic thrust, the prime benefit, or more likely, your money. Once again, not worth the risk. Why reinvent wheels when there are billions of them that can move your marketing forward?

Recently, at the conclusion of a speech I made at a national convention, I asked the audience if anyone had a guerrilla gem to impart to the assembled throng. A hand shot up. I called upon the man to speak his piece.

Repeat what works

"A *guerrilla repeats what works*," he said. "Do you agree?" Did I agree? Why do you suppose this rule is so golden?

I recall the words of Rosser Reeves, president of one of America's great advertising agencies. "Originality is the most dangerous word in advertising," he stated. You know I agree. Whenever you run a successful ad, run it *again*. Whenever you engage in a profitable promotion, engage in it *again*. Whenever you pull a high response from a direct marketing effort, repeat it *again* — and *again* and *again* and *again*. Don't walk away from blessings.

Great marketing is hard to come by. When it works for you, stay with it. If its principles have worked for others like you, go with it. Because guerrillas are far more interested in profits than originality, they abide by this golden rule in spades.

Entrepreneurial Judo

Guerrilla Marketing's Golden Rule #24:
Profits are maximized when you practice innovative marketing and protect yourself from other guerrillas.

LIFE WOULD BE glorious if you were the only marketing guerrilla in your industry. Although the nation is not teeming with guerrillas, more and more onetime greenhorn marketers are learning how to market — and how to compete against you.

Just a scant decade ago you could count on a low level of marketing sophistication among your competitors. If you had *any* marketing savvy, you had a substantial head start over the majority of your competition, which did, indeed, lack the smarts to earn serious profits through marketing. But times have changed. Marketing is more *prominent*. Data is more available. You've got to *be* a guerrilla and know how to *protect yourself against other guerrillas*.

Protect yourself

The best defense in this regard is a powerful offense. To prevent entrepreneurial judo from being used against you, the idea is to first employ it against the competition. Entrepreneurial judo means entering niches where the odds favor your success while not becoming victimized by that success when it happens. Losing your guerrilla edge makes you fodder for other guerrillas.

Business philosopher Peter Drucker alerts us to the power and effectiveness of entrepreneurial judo, which enables new companies to leapfrog over sleeping giants.

Guerrillas have employed this marketing karate whenever possible. But as more and more *new enterprises are formed*, even the most astute guerrilla must be on guard against judo being used *on the guerrilla's own company*. To do this, you must avoid bad habits that make you prey to entrepreneurial judo. Is your company likely to develop these five habits?

1. *Arrogance.* The American term for this is *NIH* — not invented here. If the innovation or idea doesn't come from the company itself, it is *automatically rejected* by the company. An outsider with a brilliant product concept doesn't have a chance of many companies producing it because *it was not theirs.* The arrogance of the American electronics industry caused the transistor to be spurned. It was NIH. It was pure corporate egotism.

2. *Creaming the market.* More than a few enterprises have decided to aim only for the high-profit segment of a market, the big users, volume buyers, top-of-the-line purchasers. They don't really ignore the little guys, but they *don't market aggressively* to them. Still, the little guys become customers eventually, and because they generally receive such poor service, they flock to competitors. Companies that neglect certain markets are vulnerable targets for judo practitioners, guerrillas ready to offer innovative service, faster delivery, flexibility. Remember that 10.8 million of America's 11 million businesses are small businesses. *Lots of cream* beneath the surface.

3. *Misunderstanding quality.* To a wet-behind-the-ears manufacturer, quality means the product was hard to make and cost a great deal of money. But that involves incompetence more than quality. Guerrilla manufacturers know that quality is *what the customer gets out of* and is willing to pay for the product, not what the manufacturer puts in. In this century one of the most glaring examples of this phenomenon was the automotive industry's boasting of its cars' large size and power when shoppers were searching for smaller cars that were economical to run.

4. *Premium prices.* Believe me, your bright competitors love it when you open the door to their judo expertise with your premium prices. For over two centuries it has been proven that a valid method of achieving higher profit margins has been *through lower costs.* What looks like higher profits to you is really an invitation for an upstart newcomer to take advantage of your delusion and steal your market share.

5. *Maximizing instead of optimizing.* When you've got a product with a limited market, you can *maximize the quality* of your product or you can *optimize the usage* by aiming it at your largest market. Xerox is an example of a company that maximized with the clearest, fastest copies. But Japanese companies used entrepreneurial judo to unseat Xerox with *simpler, lower-cost* machines. Once set in the photocopier market, they ventured into other markets. Sony started in the low end of the radio market with limited-range, inexpensive portables. The rest, as you've heard on your Walkman, is history.

Entrepreneurial judo is ideal for guerrillas because at first it sets its sights merely on *securing a stronghold.* Therefore the leaders do not defend it. Later guerrillas move forward, each time designing a product or service for a segment they will *optimize,* starting with a single beachhead.

Start with a beachhead

If you plan to use entrepreneurial judo, begin with an analysis of your industry. Investigate the producers and suppliers. Look into their policies and habits, *especially their bad habits.*

For entrepreneurial judo to work, you will be required to do some honest innovating. Generally, *it's not enough to offer the same product or same service at a lower cost.* Do what you must to give it something that elevates it from what's already out there. Newcomers must use guerrilla marketing to make themselves distinct. The tried and true leads to a dead end. I'm not talking cost; I'm talking innovation.

It is easier to practice entrepreneurial judo if you are small and low profile. If you are, you probably also have more of a penchant to take a risk and less to lose.

The trick is to employ this judo so that every effort goes into securing the highest profits. That means you are not allowed the luxury of innovation for its own sake. Everything must generate profits.

Firewood at gas stations?

One tiny company, a seller of firewood, used entrepreneurial judo to obtain giant profits. This guerrilla wanted to use judo by marketing where he would have *absolutely no competition.* He determined that a good place to sell his product would be *gas stations* where they would display it, sell it, and share in the profits. Soon hundreds of gas stations and their customers clamored for the firewood.

It was a great idea for the winter, but what about the summer? The guerrilla employed judo by selling charcoal briquets at the same gas stations. Are there any places where *you* can market with no competition? Of course there are. Determine them, then take the steps to begin enjoying the profits they'll mean, and you'll be practicing entrepreneurial judo and deriving the benefits that result from this golden rule.

The Guerrilla Marketing of Services

Guerrilla Marketing's Golden Rule #25:
Market your services successfully by capitalizing upon the bountiful opportunities to create a unique niche.

ALL OF THE fundamentals of guerrilla marketing — and then some — are pertinent to the marketing of services just as they are to the marketing of products. Both have their own specific marketing advantages, yet guerrillas relish the service sector because of the high value it places upon their imagination.

Services open opportunities to market in ways that products don't. Free demonstrations can be a powerful and low-cost weapon. Testimonials from longtime users are inexpensive and good as gold, no — better. Flip charts can demonstrate a service's benefits in a customized way.

Guerrillas around the globe provide their service free for a limited time, then try to sell it. Sampling is the equivalent technique with products. But sampling can't habituate a customer as effectively as demonstrating over a long term. How long? *Up to three months.*

Services have a *flexibility* that products lack, enabling providers to select the right positioning at the right time in the right market. By selecting a niche that is unoccupied — such as a benefit in saving time by guaranteeing a time frame — a guerrilla can have a relatively small, but immensely profitable share of market.

I've been using the same grocer for over 20 years simply because he lets me charge my purchases, giving me the freedom from checks, credit cards, and cash if I need anything from the store. Small advantages? Big to me. An urgent-care

Habituate the customer

center in Sacramento promises that patients will be seen by a professional within 20 minutes or they pay no office fee. Here, the focus is clearly upon respecting the patients' time. You can't buy that good faith for all the money in the world.

Questionnaires have extraordinary power in the hands of a guerrilla marketing any kind of service. The guerrilla learns from customers exactly what they like and don't like about the service being provided, including *a description of the service if it were to be known as the best on Earth*. From the answers come niche ideas, one after another. By committing to occupy the niche to which the customers point, the guerrilla is on course to profitably market the service. Sample guerrilla questionnaires are presented in Golden Rule #8 as well as in Chapter 8 of *Guerrilla Marketing*.

The best on Earth

If you're involved in providing services, you should know what guerrillas know about service marketing in general and about direct mail in particular since it can be such an important cog in the marketing machine. Feast your mind on these juicy tidbits on how to fatten up your service business:

- The average service company or professional practice loses *10 to 20 percent* of its customers annually due to natural attrition. Who gets those customers? Niche-players do.
- A gargantuan amount of business that comes to service firms originates through associations that might be helped by the service-provider. To get a line on the associations that you might help — and it works both ways — see the *Encyclopedia of Associations*, available in most libraries.
- To monitor competitive advertising, call SpaceTrak at 215-784-0404. They check ads in over 300 publications. It's always helpful to see how competitors in other areas advertise. If they've maintained the same campaign for over a year, they must be doing something right, right?
- Market your service with shrewdly positioned marketing, aiming for a small, specialized audience. *Four* types of Marriott hotels are why they reported a nearly 50 percent sales increase in the two years following this commitment

to a niche, or more accurately, to four niches. It's no crime to compete against yourself. It's healthy marketing.

- Gain training in *nonverbal communication*. Glen Pfau, who coached Oliver North, says there are 600,000 nonverbal gestures and only 200,000 commonly used words in the English language. Because service-providers market so successfully with direct sales presentations, get your nonverbal weapons into working order by reading up on them.

- Consider TV; attorneys report 50 to 75 new cases monthly as a result of using it. Doctors are now using it, too. TV is dynamite for communicating before-and-after stories for services. And the cost for cable TV is astonishingly low. **You may see the doctor now**

- In 1991, a sales call cost $385. At trade shows, a qualified lead runs $127. Use local trade shows to secure leads for your service.

- Add novelty items to your direct mailings. Make them directly related to your niche. Instead of one item, send a collection, one piece per week or one per month. This gives a feeling of continuity to your company, and for a service that's an important characteristic.

- Keep in mind that in your direct mail the letter gets 70 percent of your orders, the brochure gets 20 percent, the order form gets 10 percent. But *none get seen* if your outer envelope isn't opened.

- If a direct mailing is a success, it earned at least 2.2 times the money you spent on the mailing, including everything. Don't kid yourself by perpetuating mailing campaigns that fail to meet this standard. Know every penny of the cost of your mailing.

- What happens to bulk mailings? Fifty percent gets read immediately; 25 percent gets scanned; 10 percent gets set aside for later reading; 12 percent gets tossed instantly. Readers respond most to companies *they know*. The best combination for a service-provider is targeted advertising in tandem with direct marketing by mail or phone. When you mail, *they know* you. **Bulk mailing truths**

- Your audience forgets 90 percent of what it sees within two weeks; this is why repeated mailings get the best results.
- Find ways to send reminders of your services like the dentist who reminds you to have your teeth cleaned every six months. Reminders are one of the biggest advantages of marketing a service over a product. I'm floored that more people don't do it. I haven't heard from my piano tuner in years, and I haven't had my piano tuned in years. The same goes for my fireplace, which needs a chimney sweep. Ten years ago I had that work done annually because I heard from the service-providers annually. I don't look forward to those teeth-cleaning appointments, but I make them because the dentist sends a reminder — and makes a telephone follow-up, too. Just my luck — a guerrilla-marketing dentist.

My dentist, the guerrilla

Services benefit from public relations, community involvement, newsletters, and special events more than products do. Unlike products, they gain luster from positive employee attitudes. But the most potent ammunition for the service guerrilla is adhering to the golden rule of discovering and owning a niche that's yours alone.

Assuring Distribution with TV

Guerrilla Marketing's Golden Rule #26:
*It is possible to have your product sold in almost any store
you choose if you use television marketing for leverage.*

THIS RULE WAS created solely for guerrillas and wannabe
guerrillas who manufacture or distribute a product. If yours
is a service business, you'll gain only academic insight from
these pages, so I'll understand if you skip to the next rule, one
with special interest for service-providers.

But if you make something and want it to be available in
the *largest possible number of outlets frequented by your prospects,* you can achieve this heady goal by combining three
guerrilla tactics.

These tactics are necessary because of the high rate of rejection among manufacturers seeking distribution. Even when
distributors agree to place the product in stores, they can take
a percentage of the price that might make it unprofitable for
you to sell your product! Distribution is not easy to do by yourself because so many other companies are competing for the
same shelf or floor space. Many stores now charge for shelf
space by the foot. There are many ways to get distribution, but
each has its barriers. The barriers to distribution are formidable, indeed. But guerrillas succeed at obtaining distribution
with three simple tactics.

The process begins with your realizing that the cost of television advertising has dropped dramatically during the past decade; it's often even lower than radio. This is due to the rapid
growth of cable and satellite TV. *You* know that TV is now
low-priced, but most retailers don't.

So the first guerrilla tactic is to *write and produce a 30-second TV commercial* for your product. Make it a good one, with music, an announcer with a voice that inspires confidence, and impressive visuals. Of greatest importance — **A 25-second TV commercial** make it a 25-second commercial, leaving the final five seconds to show the names of the fine outlets at which your product may be purchased.

Don't spend a fortune producing your spot. Although in 1990 the average TV spot cost $193,000 to produce, great TV commercials can be produced for well under $5,000. Still, to create a desire for your product and to impress the retailers who are your potential distribution outlets, have absolutely zero touches of amateurism.

Guerrilla tactic number two: *transfer your finished commercial to an eight-millimeter format so that you or your reps can show it to outlet owners of your choosing on a handheld VCR.*

Put the store on the tube Tell the retailer that you'll run the commercial on television right in his locale, aimed at his exact audience, and you'll even mention his name and location at the end of the spot. Because of the quality you put into its creation, your commercial will whet the targeted viewers' interest in your product, and the retailer's name will be exactly what they'll be looking for.

All you want the retailer to do is to place an order for your product. Make it a sizable order because you're making an offer of great value to the retailer. The vast majority of retailers, loving the thought of having their name mentioned *on television* and dazzled because you aren't asking for one penny for shared marketing costs, will make a beeline to your dotted line so they can sign up to make their store a TV star.

After all, they know that TV commercials cost a zillion dollars to produce and a zillion more to run. They aren't guerrillas like you. Deep in their hearts, they've always wanted to be on TV, but knew they couldn't afford it.

Perhaps they even took a stab at TV in the years when a 30-second spot ran several hundred dollars and wasted most of it because the commercial aired largely to people outside their market area. Most likely, only 10 percent of the commercial's audience lived within their market area.

Those are bad numbers. No wonder retailers shy away from

TV. No wonder they'll be enthralled that you can put them on the tube again, and at no cost to them. Sure they'll place a big order for your product. The product is first-rate and so is the commercial they've just seen.

Make this arrangement with as many retail outlets as you like, but show no more than five names at the end of each commercial. If you sign up fifty retailers (which isn't difficult with the glamour and pizzazz of TV), you'll need ten five-second endings with five names on each. Run the spots alternately so that each retailer gets equal exposure.

If you'd like, ask for a mega-order and offer the retailer an exclusive for three to twelve months. Go after chains and franchises because they'll instantly see the worth and the fairness of your offer. Of course, they've probably discovered all the wonders of TV.

The third guerrilla tactic is *to create in-store signs that remind the customers in the store of the delightful product they discovered on television*. You are pulling in business with the point-of-purchase signs, and you are pushing in business with the television commercials. Good things happen to guerrillas who are willing and able to pull and push at the same time.

Signs make TV more effective

This same tactic of forcing distribution can be used with the print media, though it lacks the glamour of TV — at least in the minds of many retailers. Still, the makers of many products have become successful because they obtained distribution outlets by promising to run impressive newspaper ads that mention the outlets.

Gaining distribution with print ads

Although that tactic will never cease to be successful, a shortcut to successful print advertising is the astounding credibility that comes when your name is seen in a full-page ad in a national magazine. Create such an ad. At the bottom, put in the name of the retail outlet that you want to carry your product, along with four of its competitors.

Show the ad to the retailer and ask for a humungus order. You'll probably get it because the owner of the outlet (or chain) would be unhappy to see only the names of his competitors in such a sterling ad, especially in so prestigious a magazine. And it's not going to cost anything.

Several companies offer this ad space at a tiny portion of its rate-card price. One of them, Media Networks, Inc., a division of 3M, offers full-page ads in a galaxy of prestigious national magazines, which is no big deal until you realize that they allow you to target the ads to your specific region and pay for them at a fraction of their usual price. Call 1-800-225-3457 and ask for their media kit.

If you want a certain store or chain to carry your product, the lure of seeing their name in some of those prestigious magazines — and realizing that they didn't have to pay to put it there — is often just the ticket to getting product distribution wherever you choose. But forcing distribution is only part of the battle.

Once your product is on shelves, available to be bought, you've got to use advertising to let people know about it. Advertising promotes your product and the names of your outlets. And while this is going on, you've got to remind folks of the benefits offered in your ads by means of powerful in-store signs. This golden rule packs a three-fisted punch that commands success for you and your retailers.

The Designated Guerrilla

Guerrilla Marketing's Golden Rule #27:
Marketing will succeed only if time and energy are
regularly devoted to it by you or a person you designate.

KNOWING ALL ABOUT guerrilla marketing and not having the time to do anything about it is a waste of knowledge.

Some of the clients I've served wanted to roll up their sleeves and run the show. Others said they were paying me to protect them from the marketing process. They were too involved in operations or finance or manufacturing or engineering or administration to become involved in marketing. They knew its importance, but just plain didn't have the time to become involved. Both types of clients had what it takes to succeed in marketing — a recognition that *somebody's* got to be paying attention to it at all times.

Somebody's got to do it

We all know that marketing is a lot like flossing your teeth. It's not a whole lot of fun, but there's agony ahead if you don't do it. So too with marketing. Unless you market daily, there's going to be trouble in the form of *low or no visibility in your prospects' eyes*, and that's no way to run a company. The businesses that get into trouble are those that don't devote much attention to marketing *and* don't pay a hired gun to ride herd over the process for them.

Unless you have the time and inclination to market with verve, imagination, and intelligence, be sure you have a *designated guerrilla*. That can be a person on your payroll or an outsider, just as long as it's a person who eats, sleeps, and obsesses over your marketing.

Eats, sleeps, and obsesses

It's a person who knows that there are 100 guerrilla marketing weapons and can find a way to put 70 of them to work for you. It's a person who can take the time to create a user-friendly marketing plan that can guide your efforts over the next ten years and be understood by people with no marketing experience.

A designated guerrilla takes even more time to develop your year-long marketing calendar — a crystal ball that shows insights into your future needs in personnel, inventory, finance, and marketing.

Ideally, your designated guerrilla will approach the marketing function as all guerrillas do — with enthusiasm, confidence, high energy, a sense of joy, and a killer instinct. If not, get yourself another guerrilla.

Perhaps your designated guerrilla will be your marketing director. Possibly it will be your director of sales. It might be a marketing consultant. It might be the account supervisor at an advertising agency. And it might be you. It doesn't mean beans who it is; all that matters is that you have a good one. If you don't, you're going to miss a lot of opportunities. You'll constantly be in a position where your marketing must react rather than act. And the spirit of your company will never come shining through.

Of the many reasons for business failures, an inability to market aggressively ranks right up near the top. When that happens, the finger of fault almost always points at the CEO. That CEO is probably too busy with other business functions to give undivided attention to marketing, too egotistical to delegate the function to someone else, or too ignorant of the power of marketing to give it much thought in the first place.

Finding your guerrilla

When that's the problem, the solution is the designated guerrilla. How do you find one? The first place to look is at yourself. If you're not the answer, look within your own company at *all* of your employees. Perhaps you can spot someone who seems to have the right instincts, the right personality. An entire chapter of *Guerrilla Marketing Attack* is devoted to describing that personality.

Ask likely people if they'd enjoy the planning, launching, and maintaining of a marketing attack. Tell them what's involved. Are they willing to learn about marketing? The science, art, and business of marketing *can* be learned; you don't have to be a born guerrilla.

There are books, seminars, newsletters, courses, and audio cassettes that can give a bright person more solid and realistic information about marketing than four years of study at a university that teaches Dark Ages tactics for companies with million-dollar budgets. Once a person is no longer intimidated by the very thought of marketing — because it's too nebulous for most people — he might get excited at the thought of becoming a five-star designated guerrilla.

This person must understand that the job of a designated guerrilla is neither a full-time nor a part-time job. The time necessary transcends standard definitions. Sometimes it's a raft of time, other times a sliver.

How much time will be demanded?

Either way, it is a *very important job*, and it does take time. How much time? You've just got to do it to find out. The most time will be demanded at the outset, when a lot of planning is done. Less time will be required during the launch phase, when the weapons are put into motion. And still less time — but *constant* time — must be put in as you sustain the attack.

That time will be devoted to three things.

1. Maintaining the marketing efforts
2. Tracking the marketing efforts
3. Developing improved marketing efforts

This does not take all day every day. The designated guerrilla will spend *some time* doing these three things, but that person can also carry another title and other responsibilities. The designated guerrilla, if chosen from within, may also be a salesperson, secretary, or supervisor. The person can do that work and also activate and energize your marketing, make it happen and make it work.

The designated guerrilla is one of the most important jobs in your business. If you're not one and can't find one in your firm, select an outsider. To follow this golden rule, make sure it's a person or agency that shares your vision and is a potential guerrilla.

Strategic Alliances

Guerrilla Marketing's Golden Rule #28:
To assure your marketing success in the future, become more oriented to cooperation than competition.

AS THE OWNER of a business that engages in marketing, you're out there amidst the competition all by yourself. It costs more to operate that way. And your options, as a loner, are more limited. So is the service you are able to provide. This is not good in an era when customers require more than ever in the way of coddling and follow-through.

The *strategic alliance* is your solution for the 1990s and beyond. Businesses that flourish will not be independent firms

The end of the one-man band

as characterized by the age of the one-man-band entrepreneur. Instead, they'll be *dependent firms* that need one another to prosper as small, or even gigantic, businesses.

These firms will depend upon others for expertise, money, people, service, and the way the world perceives them. The dependence will be manifested in the form of strategic alliances. *The strategy is to increase profits.*

Unlike standard partnerships and other joint ventures, strategic alliances will be as much for the short term as for the long term. Think profit, not marriage.

Who will be your allies?

With whom will you engage in these strategic alliances?

- Suppliers
- Competitors from your own area
- Competitors from distant areas
- Businesses with the same audience
- Businesses in your community
- Businesses on your street
- Huge national businesses

- Private investors
- Your personnel
- Your bank
- Your landlord
- Your service providers

The key to establishing and maintaining strategic alliances will be *cooperation* rather than *competition*. The guerrilla's goal: a network of contacts and colleagues and co-strivers, all helping their profits by building yours.

Consistent success and growth will belong to teams and not to players. They will possess a strength and durability not dreamed of by the lone wolf entrepreneur.

Teams, not players

Strategic alliances combine the essential ingredients of a successful business: planning, marketing, technology, inventory, humans, and money. That's a lot of ingredients, so it may take several allies to form slam-dunk strategic alliances.

Your allies will provide new value to your business. That value pumps up your financing power. So if you think a strategic alliance is a method of obtaining funds for a business, you've got it right. Anyone who grants you those funds — lending institution, private investor, venture capitalist — will be your ally.

The bull's-eye to aim for is always *the success of the alliance*. If it is successful, the small businesses within it will be successful. With the proper allies, small business success rates will soar.

One of the most potent guerrilla marketing weapons, fusion marketing, embodies the very spirit of a strategic alliance. By combining marketing efforts, alliances are able to increase their marketing exposure while decreasing their marketing costs. No wonder fusion marketing is so popular in Japan. Consider these real-life examples:

Real-life alliances

- In Nagoya, Japan, you'll find a combination bookstore, variety store, haberdashery, used-car lot, and used-motorcycle lot. There's an alliance for you.
- In Osaka, the fusion of a pool hall, bookstore, bowling

alley, video shop, film developer, and noodle restaurant proves that alliances are not always obvious.

- In Hiratsuka, the strategic alliance is between a car dealer, family restaurant, ice cream parlor, and convenience store. Walk in, drive out — well-fed and well-stocked.
- In Tokyo, combined allies include an athletic club, beauty shop, aesthetic salon, and a dentist. Look further and you'll find the gas station that allocates shelf space to a video shop, floor space to a café, wall space to an art gallery, and outside space to a used-car dealer.
- In the United States, Disney and Lucasfilms have teamed up with soft-drink companies and fast-food operations for many promotions. These alliances aren't merely limited to big-name companies here. Tie-ins are springing up in local communities from coast to coast, with small businesses climbing aboard the bandwagon for mutual marketing efforts.

These examples from Japan involve geographic proximity and shared real estate expenses. But that is not always necessary, merely a winning by-product of cooperation versus competition.

Partnerism   In the book *Guerrilla Financing*, co-authored by Bruce Blechman and me, we call this phenomenon "partnerism," and we define partnerism as "combining all the necessary resources to make a business successful." A key point we stress is that *you must consider everyone you deal with on a business basis as your partner — as a potential ally for a strategic alliance.* If you've had bad luck with partners in the past, relegate that experience to the past because it has zilch to do with the future. Partners are happening now and will continue to happen. Join in.

You'll discover partnerships couched in terms such as strategic alliances, fusion marketing, tie-ins, or collaborative marketing. You'll see it practiced by big guys such as Disney and McDonald's, Kmart and Little Caesar's Pizza restaurant chain, Pathe Films and Bantam Books, Pepto-Bismol and H&R Block, Timex and Kodak, Apple and IBM, Ford and Mazda.

Those last two combinations are alliances between competitors! Strategic alliances are not that new an idea. When Thomas Edison formed a strategic alliance with Corning Glass, the ball started rolling. Or should I say the bulb?

To spot likely alliances for your company, look at the eight major components of these alliances: marketing, logistics, packaging, pricing, product design, selling, service, and geographic proximity. These are spokes that come from a central hub — at the alliance strategy.

Eight major components

The potential complexity of a collaboration is one of its greatest strengths because *it is difficult to copy or compete with* — giving you a built-in competitive edge.

Get the knack for spotting sensible and potentially lucrative strategic alliances. In time, they'll become obvious to you, and you'll realize that the most profitable alliances aren't always the first ones that come to mind. The imagination of the guerrilla is indispensable in this area.

That's why the guerrilla knows that today is a good day to start alliance-shopping and following this golden rule to future success.

Part Three

Golden Rules to Guide Your Marketing Materials

Competitive Advantages

Guerrilla Marketing's Golden Rule #29:
Identify or create your competitive advantages, then concentrate your marketing upon them.

MANY OF TODAY'S products and services are so similar to each other that their only difference is their marketing. They try to woo new customers with jingles, special effects, and fancy production.

These marketing devices are desperate solutions for people with limited imaginations. Although there is little question that they can help, a serious guerrilla knows there are other marketing weapons that are far more potent.

Among the most important of these weapons are *competitive advantages*. If your widget doubles a company's profitability, grows hair on bald heads, or attracts lifelong love partners, you don't have to use special effects. Jingles will get in the way of clarity. Just the truth will do very nicely, thank you. It is said that you don't have to wound a charging tiger all over; one well-placed shot will do the job.

Perhaps you have a plethora of competitive advantages. The only ones that can be translated into instant profits are the marketable ones, the kind that are natural fodder for market- **Are they** ing. A new kind of fabricating material, unless it is a dramatic **marketable?** advancement, will probably only bore your prospects. But a toothpaste that eliminates plaque, cavities, and bad breath, while whitening teeth at the same time, can be marketed with a high expectation of success.

The idea is to *identify* your marketable competitive advantages, then *stress* them in all of your marketing. If you don't have any marketable competitive advantages, you've got to realize that a smart guerrilla creates them by improving his product or service or both.

The area most fertile for creating a new competitive advantage is *service*. There are gobs of gardeners in my area. All charge about the same price, do about the same job. But why did I switch my business to Gonzalez Silent Gardening? *Because they specialize in gardening quietly and use no noisy implements.* That's an important benefit to my wife and me. Noise doesn't rob me of one second of my writing time while Gonzalez is hard at work. My wife can sleep late even while gardeners are outside the bedroom window. This competitive advantage won our appreciation and our business.

Invent your advantage

Gonzalez surveyed the competitive scene, then invented his competitive advantage and advertised it. That's exactly what I'm recommending to you.

- If you run a dry cleaning business, offer pickup and delivery.
- If you run a baby-sitting service, offer a healthy snack in addition to the expected meal.
- If you make holiday baskets, give people the freedom to create their own baskets from a selection of gift items.
- If you sell computer hardware, offer free service for the first year, with regular checkups as part of the package.
- If you are an accountant, offer tax consultations for $300, but free to your existing clients.

You can see that competitive advantages mean offering a better value, and sometimes requiring extra work or a free offer from you. But investments in competitive advantages are frequently the wisest investments a business can make.

See what your competitors are offering. Patronize them if you can. Keep a sharp eye for areas in which you can surpass them, especially in service. Perhaps you can offer faster delivery, on-site services, gift wrapping, more frequent follow-up, maintenance for a period of time, installation, a longer guarantee, an extra service, training, shipping, free companion items, the possibilities are endless. Each may be worth a fortune to you.

It may be that you already have a competitive advantage that is not recognized as such. Back in the 1930s, a copywriter went for a tour of the Lucky Strike cigarette factory. When he entered a large, warm room filled with tobacco, he asked the tour leader what went on in that room.

"Nothing really, that's just our toasting room," said the tour leader. "Do all cigarette companies have toasting rooms?" asked the canny copywriter. "Sure, they all do" was the answer.

But no other company was marketing them. The writer suggested that Luckies say "It's toasted!" right on the package and in all the advertisements. The Lucky Strike marketing director complied, and soon the brand became America's number-one seller — using a competitive advantage not recognized as such by their competition . . . or even by themselves!   **Invisible advantages**

Such stories are legion. The important thing is to identify or create your own, then ride it to victory.

Examples of companies that fail to rely upon their competitive advantages abound. They have the fastest, quietest, or most energy-conserving product or service, yet in their marketing they talk about their price or their style. *Anybody* can talk about price or style. But only one can be the fastest, quietest, or most energy-conserving.

Because of the enormous clutter in marketing messages, I'm tempted to suggest that you concentrate *solely* upon your competitive advantages and upon nothing else. But some items beyond competitive advantages do require marketing.

Your marketing can mention competitors' names when making comparisons, but be sure you're telling the truth. **Making** Sometimes these comparisons can bring out a competitive **comparisons** advantage.

Once you have selected the most compelling of your competitive advantages, find how to make it the prime topic of your ads, brochures, mailings, commercials, videos, sales presentations, and telemarketing efforts. The selection process should *measure the competitive advantages by five yardsticks*:

clarity, uniqueness, desirability, believability, and motivation. The five questions to ask are

1. Will my target market perceive this as an advantage?
2. Is this different from what competitors offer?
3. Will people honestly benefit from this advantage?
4. Will they believe my statement about the advantage?
5. Does this advantage motivate them to buy now or soon?

Unless you can give five resounding "yeses" in answer to these questions, get yourself another competitive advantage to hang your marketing upon.

Because you're going to lean with all your weight upon your competitive advantage, be certain it's a strong one. Small guerrilla companies have an edge over the big guys in this arena because their flexibility enables them to create service advantages in a hurry and carve out profitable niches. Big guerrilla companies have an edge over small businesses because their financial muscle allows them to create product advantages. They know that an investment in a marketable product advantage is part of the marketing budget and a sagacious way to invest money.

A wise investment

Although many products and services appear to be similar, the guerrilla discovers many differences, and then determines which of the differences are true competitive advantages. In the unlikely case that the offerings *are* extremely similar, the guerrilla *creates* differences that yield clear competitive advantages. Then the guerrilla follows this golden rule as a path for all marketing.

The Mighty Headline

Guerrilla Marketing's Golden Rule #30:
*If you have ten hours to spend creating an ad, spend nine
of them on the headline.*

PEOPLE WILL MAKE the decision to read or ignore your newspaper or magazine ad primarily because of your headline. If
the rest of your ad is a winner, but the headline is a loser, you
are making a major marketing blunder.

Guerrillas stay ahead of their competitors by utilizing state-
of-the-moment information and technology. But the basics
are never left behind. For ads, brochures, signs, direct mail,
and a multitude of other marketing weapons, your headline
dictates your positioning in the mind of your prospect — and
attracts prospect attention or apathy. It is the most important
thing you say to the prospect.

When a guerrilla thinks in terms of headlines, the thinking
process takes him directly to newspapers, then magazines,
then brochures. Guerrillas also know that just as important
as headlines — but different because of the environment in
which they are used — are opening lines: to radio spots, TV
commercials, direct mail letters, telemarketing calls, and several other marketing weapons. These are different, but no less
important. Just keep in mind that you've got three seconds to
capture the attention of your viewer or listener. Do it then or
not at all.

Although much of marketing is riddled with exceptions,
and the upcoming guidelines have more than their fair share,
you are on the right track if you begin by knowing what the
guerrilla knows about creating powerful headlines.

Tracing the roots of modern marketing, the guerrilla en-
counters formulas for writing headlines. They still make sense.

*The most
important thing
you say*

*Formulas for
writing headlines*

Here are 20 hints and options, based upon these formulas, for your future headlines:

1. Realize that your headline must either *convey an idea* or *intrigue the reader* into wanting to read more of your writing.
2. Speak *directly to the reader,* one reader at a time, even if 20 million people will read your headline.
3. Write your headline in news style.
4. Use words that have an announcement quality.
5. Experiment with headlines that begin with "Announcing."
6. Experiment with headlines that begin with "New."
7. Put a date in your headline.
8. Feature the price — if you're proud of it — in your headline. It need not be a low price for the ad to succeed.
9. Feature an easy payment plan.
10. Announce a free offer.
11. Offer information of value.
12. Start to tell a story.
13. Begin your headline with "How to."
14. Begin your headline with "How," "Why," "Which," "You," or "This."
15. Begin your headline with "Advice."
16. Use a testimonial-style headline.
17. Offer the reader a test.
18. Use a one-word headline.
19. Warn the reader not to delay buying.
20. Address your headline to a specific person. (Remember when I needed that first business suit? Every day there are specific individuals who want exactly what you're offering.)

In almost every case, if the reader *isn't stopped* by your headline, that reader will move on to something else, and it won't be more of your advertisement. What a waste! Your heart was in the right place because you were investing in marketing.

But your investment was mismanaged by your failure to properly judge a basic part of your marketing.

Many companies use remarkably effective computer software, but waste marketing dollars with woefully inept headlines. Headlines and opening lines are your *initial bonds* to your prospects. They must do one of two things for you: (1) Make an offer that leads to the sale, or (2) Intrigue the reader into wanting to learn more. Equally important as saying something cogent is *the manner in which you say it*.

What headlines must do

Boring and indirect headlines sabotage thoughtful copy and brilliant graphics every day. Marvelous offers are not accepted by a ready public because the headline fell down on the job. There are more bad than good headlines in every edition of every newspaper.

More bad ones than good ones

In such an atmosphere, guerrillas thrive. They appreciate headlines that do not draw attention away from their own efforts. Their headlines get noticed, generate readership, attract responses, and result in profits.

Although a company probably cannot achieve greatness solely based upon the headlines in its marketing materials, without solid headlines, its growth will be impeded. Your job may be to create headlines or to judge them. It is one of your most important jobs.

To gain a better perspective on their headlines, guerrillas paste mock-ups of their ad, complete with headline (but not necessarily the copy), into a copy of their daily newspaper. In this way they can compare it with the other headlines in the paper and are better able to detect its strengths and weaknesses.

The extra time and money it takes to do this — and it doesn't take much of either — are a worthy investment that will help you follow this golden rule about the awesome might and power of a headline.

Magic Words
and Tragic Words

Guerrilla Marketing's Golden Rule #31:
The right words will propel a great idea toward success;
the wrong words will doom a great idea to failure.

ALTHOUGH EVERYONE knows that a great idea must be expressed with great words, not everyone knows those words. But guerrillas become aware of more of them each year, and if you enrich your marketing vocabulary with magic words, your financial statements may begin to show magic numbers.

Guerrilla marketing is concerned not only with *what you say* in your marketing, but also with *how you say it*. Saying the right thing with the wrong words is a waste of time and money, not to mention a very preventable error.

One of the more intriguing aspects of the magic words is their *durability*. Hard-nosed marketers have been using many of these words since the turn of the century. Most of the words have been established and verified in everyday usage since Day One of marketing, yet they maintain their magic. "I love you" will never sound trite.

"I love you"

Certain words have the power to turn prospects on and to motivate them to think the right thoughts. Other words have the power to turn prospects off and to motivate them to think thoughts detrimental to your business.

As a guerrilla, you know that it doesn't matter whether or not you are writing or saying these words, but it matters like crazy that you have a *built-in alarm system* for the magic and tragic words. That system must ring and flash in your head the moment you encounter one of the tragic words in your marketing. It must also recognize the absence of magic words. Sure, it's possible to write potent marketing copy without magic words. It's also possible to walk from New York to San Francisco on your knees. Why bother if there are better ways to get where you want to be?

In my book *Guerrilla Marketing* I wrote about the magic words. The list has grown as more guerrillas have shared their findings. Right now, meaning in this era as much as at this moment, the magic words — with the most important words first — are

FREE	LOVE	SAFE
NEW	BENEFITS	RIGHT
YOU	ALTERNATIVE	SECURITY
SALE	NOW	WINNINGS
INTRODUCING	WIN	FUN
SAVE	GAIN	VALUE
MONEY	HAPPY	ADVICE
DISCOVER	TRUSTWORTHY	WANTED
RESULTS	GOOD-LOOKING	ANNOUNCING
EASY	COMFORTABLE	YOUR
PROVEN	PROUD	PEOPLE
GUARANTEED	HEALTHY	WHY

These words carry far more than the weight of one word. **Heavyweight words** *Use them.* Put them in your advertising, in your brochures, on your signs, in your letters, in your telemarketing, wherever you can. They describe what people want. They make people read on. They offer things that people are looking for.

As there are magic words that can speed you on the way to your goal, there are tragic words that can impede you. There's no need to use these customer-stopping words. But, of course, business owners use them every day. Non-guerrillas know well the pain of marketing that didn't pull. But few of them know that one tiny word may have made the difference.

So as not to be a word abuser, stay on the alert for the tragic **Word alert!** words:

BUY	DIFFICULT	DEATH
OBLIGATION	WRONG	ORDER
FAILURE	DECISION	FAIL
BAD	DEAL	COST
SELL	LIABILITY	WORRY
LOSS	HARD	CONTRACT

These words, too, are more powerful than other words in the language. They make readers lose interest, stop reading. They can undermine your marketing effort.

The magic words aren't necessarily marketing words, but they should be whenever possible. When blended with new words, expressing ideas about your company, the magic words give new power to your marketing.

Word use and customer tracking have determined that the magic words are the most persuasive words in the English language. A study of 100 famous profit-producing headlines is replete with these words. I predict *fast* will soon join the list.

There are also magic phrases that persuade people to see it your way, desire it, buy it. Some of these are *limited time offer, 50% discount, haircut & shampoo $8.00, custom-made, this month only, supplies limited to stock on hand only*, and many more that I'm sure you know well. Remember, as increasing **The most** numbers of marketers do, that the most readable words in the **readable phrase** language, the most enjoyable to listen to, the ones with the maxi-magic to capture attention and readership, are *the reader's name*. It is difficult to overuse these words.

The idea in marketing is not to shun magic words in a mindless search for originality, but to use them for their pull and proven ability to generate profits. The key word in that sentence is "proven" because that's the quality that gives the words their marketing magic.

Undoubtedly, there are more beautiful words in the language, but in marketing *beautiful* only relates to the looks of your financial statement.

As a guerrilla with plans to stay and succeed in business, it **Keep an** makes sense to keep an eagle eye out for new magic words. **eagle eye** You won't be able to spot them instantly, but over time they will become apparent to the trained eye. So start training yours. Keep a list of the words that excite you, entice you.

There is not a lot in marketing that guarantees success. Many things have worked before, but haven't yet established staying power. Marketing is littered with words that died and led to the tragic demise of many marketing campaigns simply because the words were trendy or faddish. Trends and fads have this ungainly habit of dying, and with them in many cases expensive marketing bites the dust.

Whenever you can go with something that has been *proven by time to produce results for marketing investments* — and believe me, you won't have many of those — jump at the opportunity. Because magic in marketing is so hard to come by, use it when you can. It's just as easy to say "agreement" as "contract." In fact, there's a golden rule that urges you to do so.

Humanity in Marketing

Guerrilla Marketing's Golden Rule #32:
Realize that everyone to whom you market is a human being first and a customer next.

GUERRILLAS KNOW that it is crucial to make the human bond before you can make a lasting business bond. To avoid the depersonalization that has been an unpleasant side effect of the computer age and rampant within the business community, several guerrilla marketing weapons may be employed to add more humanity to your marketing process and more profits to your till.

On the retail level, it means using the weapons of a warm smile, clear eye contact, and whenever possible (think of ways to make it possible), using the person's name. That feels human. That feels comfortable. That makes the person feel good. And good feelings can lead to high profits.

Make people feel good

Naturally, this should also be your modus operandi during trade shows, whether you're an exhibitor or a browser. Throwing parties for key customers and prospects at trade shows has been a wise investment for companies that want to warm up their human relations.

The personality of your company, as heard on the telephone, can turn your customers and prospects on — or turn them off. If you absolutely must put callers on hold, let them hear good music and interesting news about your company, especially special offers or new offerings. Messages as long as two minutes have proven to be effective when used in this manner. If the information is interesting, the callers will not be put off. Be sure to thank callers for their patience.

If you must keep them on hold longer than two minutes, and you're no guerrilla if you're guilty of this, install a phone system that redirects their calls quickly and politely. Don't keep them waiting without explanation or feeling ignored.

All time spent interacting with the customer should be oriented to serving the customer's needs and to saving the customer's time. A good way to strengthen the human bond with the customer is to make the purchasing process as simple as possible. The idea is to be easy to do business with.

Accept all credit cards. Provide partial payment plans. Offer overnight delivery. Encourage telephone ordering. Do the necessary sales training, usually every week if you're taking marketing seriously, to be sure your sales and service reps are articulate, pleasant, and a reflection of your company's identity.

Your prospects have to buy you before they buy what you're selling. They have to buy your representatives before they buy what they're selling. A sincerely humane approach warms up **Warm it up** what could have been a cold business transaction. And it motivates the customer to become a repeat customer and to give your company good word-of-mouth.

Add humanity by asking questions, listening closely to the answers, wanting to be of maximum service to the customer, providing free data in the form of brochures, newsletters, videotapes, the full gamut of guerrilla marketing weapons.

Make warmth and humanity part of your written marketing **Part of your** plan. That plan should have a statement of your identity, not **strategy** some false image, but an honest identity. Your employees should read the marketing plan — easy to do with a seven-sentence guerrilla marketing plan — so that they can carry forth your banner of human recognition. Treat your employees the way you want them to treat your customers and good feeling will be contagious throughout your company.

This attitude costs nary a cent, yet is a weapon of marketing. So is the enthusiasm, another free and potent weapon, displayed by your employees. Speaking of employees, your humanity should extend throughout your company as well as throughout your customer list. Just remember that human re- **HR is PR** lations are simply public relations in their highest form.

Realize that we are leaving the old cold world of broadcasting and entering the new warm world of narrowcasting. You should try not to say everything to everybody but to say something to somebody. The more you treat marketing as a one-on-one process rather than a method of mass selling, the more humanity will be in your marketing and the more profits in your bank account.

To succeed at injecting humanity into your marketing, you must become an expert. An expert on what? An expert on your customers, on their needs, their problems, their desires, their goals, even their personal likes and dislikes. Believe me, your customers will be amazed when you treat them like human beings rather than like members of a demographic group.

Your focus should be on your customers' goals as well as your own. That means your job is to build lasting relationships and to earn the confidence of your prospects. The more your marketing is individualized rather than generalized, the more on-target it will be. Orient your marketing to the things on your customers' and prospects' minds rather than the things on your mind. That's really what humanity is all about.

To add humanity, you'll have to become an active listener as well as a specialist in your customers. You'll have to be a warm, caring human before you're a guerrilla marketer. Will **Will customers** your customers and prospects notice this attitude? Wouldn't **notice?** you notice it if any business entity began to treat you more as a person than a profit source? Because very few do, your company will stand out when you put humanity into your marketing.

Humanity does not mean flattering, complimenting, or buttering up. It means wanting to help, wanting the very things for your customers that they want for themselves. A wondrous side benefit is the more you can get your customers to talk about themselves, the more they'll tell you and the more you'll learn about ways you can help.

Your goal as a guerrilla will be to become liked, trusted, believed, and relied upon. Of course, your goal will also be to generate profits for your company. In the coming decades, that will be most easily accomplished if you can generate profits for your customers. Your growth should come from their growth. That's the healthiest kind of growth in the business world.

You should select your salespeople for their ability to establish rapport rather than to close sales, for their ability to make friends rather than to make presentations. Of course, they'll need the normal sales skills, but a knowledge of human behavior will be their key to success. And a sincere desire to get to know their customer *on a personal basis* will help them ring up more sales than any flip chart or sales aid. You'll be seeing more and more humanity in marketing as we approach the twenty-first century. The guerrilla will be the person who leads rather than follows this trend by following this golden rule in all marketing.

Humor in Marketing

Guerrilla Marketing's Golden Rule #33:
Avoid the use of humor unless it is pertinent to your offering and does not detract from your offer.

IF YOU'RE MARKETING a comedy club, a comedy album, a comedian, or a book of jokes, humor might be just the ticket for you — because people will remember the humor in your marketing. And that's just what you want them to remember.

But if you're marketing something other than those items, unless it's an inexpensive offering such as chewing gum, candy, a kids' product, a funny movie, or a snack item, humor **A leech** can be a leech — sucking away interest and attention from your product or service. People, being people, will remember the humor of your marketing, not the idea you want them to remember. And there's very little chance that they'll remember your product or service.

Too many marketing creators believe that marketing is supposed to be funny, to make people laugh. Many marketing directors worship at this same altar of wit, not wisdom.

As a result, many of today's radio and TV commercials, plus a generous dollop of print ads and even brochures, are more humorous than they are effective. Sure, they make prospects feel good, but that good feeling isn't necessarily connected to your company. The company takes a back seat.

Worse yet, even wonderful humor isn't funny when it's repeated. How many times do you want to hear a joke? Yet supposedly sophisticated companies pay small fortunes for TV or radio campaigns that are hilarious the first time you see or hear them, amusing the second time, embarrassing the third, and grating thereafter.

Repetition is necessary to assure the effectiveness of mar-

keting. But humor loses its punch with repetition. It's a joy in **Loses its punch**
many forms, but a disaster to the people picking up the tab for
marketing.

As a famed antacid garnered awards for its side-splitting
commercials about "spicy meatballs" — "I can't believe I ate
the *whole thing!*" — sales of the product took a tumble. It
seemed that folks didn't want a belly laugh when it came to
buying something for their bellyache.

Now that I've got you thinking seriously about humor, let
me give you official permission to use humor in your marketing. But be sure to use it intelligently and always connect it to
your product.

Bartles and Jaymes has used humor brilliantly. So has Mil-
ler Lite. Volkswagen did in the past. But the list *does not* go
on and on. And some of these companies have since aban-
doned humor as the cornerstone of their marketing thrust.

Some marketing — direct or otherwise — uses humor to
introduce a topic, succeeding admirably at attracting attention. But then the marketing switches to a more somber note.
The reader feels disillusioned. I call this the "Speaking-of-
Insects-How's-Your-Aunt?" school of marketing. Shun it.

Humor is at best a dangerous weapon in the marketing
wars. It is frequently misused, rarely required, and soon resented. Yet it does break barriers — especially in telemarketing. It does create favorable association. It does break from the
pack if the pack is boring, as it usually is. Humor is not inher- **Humor is not**
ently bad in marketing. It's how people use it that makes it **inherently bad**
bad, transforms it into that insatiable leech. It's very tough to
use it correctly.

Never resort to humor as a cheap substitute for describing
the solid benefits offered by your product or service. People do
enjoy reading and seeing funny things, it's true. But even
more, they enjoy reading and seeing things about themselves.

Marketing people who are unable to find something interesting to say about the reader or viewer, unable to spot a major
benefit of their offering, unable to come up with the primary
reasons people should make the purchase, unable to create a
powerful desire to buy — those are the ones who resort to hu-

mor. Not because humor is the right way to market, but because humor is the only thing they could find to make their point.

When your entire company is riding on your marketing, it is foolhardy to risk the future of that company on a joke. Yet jokes are the common dead end streets the unimaginative travel in marketing.

One of the most compelling reasons to follow this golden rule is that humor *gets in the way of repetition*, and repetition is the way to gain share of mind. If prospects are going to turn off their minds when they are exposed to your humorous marketing for the umpteenth time, you have succeeded in making repetition work *against* you. That's like having a Patriot missile and aiming it at your bellybutton.

Gets in the way of repetition

Even if you are deeply committed to your marketing, if your marketing materials are humor-oriented, people will long remember your humor before they remember the reasons to buy your product. Remember, marketing is supposed to create a desire to buy. Humor creates a desire to giggle. There's an enormous gap between spending and giggling.

There's a fine line between lightheartedness and humor. Levi's 501 marketing has always been lighthearted, but it has never given anyone a major chuckle. The California Raisins are lovable and cheerful characters, but they're not rib-tickling. They're out for your money, not your laughs.

Monitor yourself

Let your personal experience help you understand this rule. When you see marketing that makes you laugh, see if it makes you want to purchase the product or service being marketed. See if you can easily remember the advertiser. See how long you can even pay attention to the marketing before it begins to turn you off. Take a close look at humor through the eyes of a profit-minded marketer.

It's okay to make people smile, laugh, feel good about you. But it's not okay to do this at the expense of your overall marketing premise. And that premise probably has little to do with obtaining grins and guffaws. Banks don't accept those or deposit them to your account.

You don't want people to tell you how funny your marketing is. You want them to tell you how much they want whatever it is you are marketing. Let them get their laughs from TV shows, movies, and comedy clubs. That's the job of those forums. It is *not* the job of marketing. That's why avoiding humor is a golden rule.

The Value of Specifics

Guerrilla Marketing's Golden Rule #34:
The believability and persuasion of your marketing increase in direct proportion to how much specific data you provide.

IF YOU OFFER the highest quality, best service, and lowest price, it doesn't mean a thing if people don't believe you. When you are engaged in the act of marketing — any of the 100 acts — you are up against an automatic believability barrier. The guerrilla's mission: surmount the barrier. The way to succeed: with specifics that force believability.

Suppose you are an athletic director at a local school. You receive a letter from a fund-raising company that starts out, "Last month the athletic department at Sherman Elementary School, here in Chicago six blocks away from your school, raised $3,968 in just three days."

Specifics hit home
A letter with an opening like that is going to hit home with you because it uses the power of specifics and targeted marketing. When the letter concludes by offering you a chance to call a toll-free number or to write for a free brochure on how your school can do what Sherman Elementary did, there's a good chance you'll call or write.

One of America's leading fund-raising companies attained its leadership position by targeting that specifically and being that specific in its direct mailings. Names and numbers were high-potency weapons for this firm.

There is no question that *information* — in the form of specific data — is a guerrilla marketing weapon *if you use it*. Having the info and not marketing with it is wasting a weapon. My book *Guerrilla Marketing Weapons* calls the information weapon "research" because that's the source of most specifics.

Specifics have the ability to *convince* people more than anything else that what you are saying is true. Specifics *prove* what your words say. If you say you're a fine fund-raising company and talk about your commitment to service and success, that's not nearly as cogent as mentioning names and numbers that will be meaningful to your prospects.

Convince and prove

The more names, the better. The more numbers, the better. Don't quote all names and numbers — only those that will most match up with your prospect. But have a lot for back-up support.

Specifics have enormous value to your company when you are *setting goals*. Rather than saying you will increase sales, say you will increase them by 2 percent a month, even half a percent a month. State that figure in dollars and *put it in writing*. The power of that single specific can be the difference between success and failure.

I am flabbergasted when I encounter companies that fail to quantify their goals. They set growth goals that call for consistent monthly growth rather than 3 percent growth per month — a quantified, specified goal rather than some vague target. You can help companies by helping them to be specific.

When dealing with prospect companies, talk to them in terms of specific profits. Tell them *how their profits will increase, then proceed to prove it to them by using numbers, even hypothetical numbers*. To be a guerrilla, you must move beyond words and into facts. Facts are specific.

When making claims for your product or service, give a *step-by-step* proof of its efficacy. Show why it is good. Use *case histories* as much as possible. Successful case histories will pack more punch than the glossiest of brochures and the glitziest of commercials. If your software helped a bookstore in Nashville triple its profits, you can be sure that bookstores in Seattle will want to know about it, too. What bookstore wouldn't?

Case histories

A case history of a company that closely resembles your prospect in size, age, or type of industry is ultrapowerful and should be a highlight of your marketing to that prospect. I know of one company whose primary marketing weapon is a loose-leaf notebook filled with case histories. True guerrilla marketing. It costs hardly anything, but convinces with million-dollar persuasion. Show photos of work you've done, especially before-and-after shots. That's about as specific as you can get.

On the same level as case histories are real-life *examples*. Perhaps you aren't able to provide the whole breakdown of the experience, but you can show examples of companies or families or individuals benefiting from what you offer. Lean on these examples. Each one is a specific, more irrefutable proof of what you say. Each helps you leap over the believability barrier — even helps disintegrate it.

As you can use "what if" situations to prove your case about profits, you can use hypothetical examples to help make your points. Real examples are the best, but use pretend examples if no real-life ones come to mind. These are called scenarios and usually begin with the words "Suppose there was a company such as yours that tried what we're offering. Suppose they invested . . ." You get the idea.

Testimonials are specific

In the same category as case histories, examples, and scenarios — just as powerful and equally inexpensive — are *testimonials*. Are they specific? Does a bear do what a bear does in the forest?

Again, many guerrilla companies compile testimonial letters and put them into a handsome leather loose-leaf binder. Each sales rep has a binder filled with testimonials — and each is responsible for obtaining six more during the course of a year. Eventually, binders can be created for targeted markets: parents, computer users, small businesses, whatever your guerrilla heart desires. For many companies these binders become the single most important marketing weapon. And their profits must be ridiculously high because their marketing investment is so low.

Specifics apply to other areas of customer relations as well. The invitation "Let's have lunch sometime" is probably going to leave two people hungry. "Let's have lunch this Friday, the twentieth, at twelve noon at the India Village" — that's going to feed the folks.

Specifics also include lists — the names of clients and customers you have served, the number of years you've been in business, the exact services you offer, your prices, the ways you differ from competitors, your competitive advantages, awards won, publicity earned, and ways the prospect can benefit by making the purchase from you right now.

I say "right now" because you want to set a date for the customer to buy from you, and "right now" seems like the most preferable from your point of view. If you must say "next Monday the twenty-third," that's okay, too. It's much better than "one of these days soon." But it's not as okay as "right now."

Specifics about your prospect are equally valuable. Asking prospects about them can help immensely in closing the sale. Statements like "I like the color green" and "Wednesday the twenty-fifth would be the best delivery day" are music to a guerrilla's ears. Follow this golden rule and make beautiful music.

Marketing Combinations

Guerrilla Marketing's Golden Rule #35:
Many marketing weapons attain their maximum effectiveness only when combined with other weapons of marketing.

A CLIENT OF MINE who uses a lot of telemarketing was satisfied with his telemarketing results, but wondered if he could reach more people in less time. His business was a video rental operation that operated without a store. Customers were given a directory of movies, and a lock-box was installed on their houses. If they wanted to rent a movie, they called a number and the movie was delivered. When they had viewed it, they put it in the lock-box. No time wasted going to and from a video store.

Because of the ridiculously low cost of cable television, we decided to experiment with direct response television, using a 30-second rather than the usual 120-second spot. The spots were scripted, produced, and run. Everyone who saw them before they aired thought they would be successful. They made a complex story simple. They made their pitch visually as well as verbally. And they offered a special gift to viewers who called in and ordered the product *now.* Just as important, they were run at peak viewing times on shows tailored for the target audience.

But, in spite of this careful planning, very few people phoned in to buy and take advantage of the gift offer. At first, **Bad news** this made my client one unhappy dude, especially since this **for my client** was his first foray into mass media.

Later my client called me sounding very excited. Was it because the TV commercials started to elicit orders? Nope. It was because *his telemarketing results more than tripled.* Many of the people his staff called mentioned, in response to a specific question, that they had seen the TV spots but just didn't pick up the phone.

Instead, the TV spots worked in the classic manner of television, *promoting a change of attitude* and preselling a service. They didn't generate instant sales like standard direct response marketing. But the television investment more than paid for itself in increased business.

Good news for my client

Because of this my client, now a confirmed guerrilla and no longer intimidated by mass media, changed the TV spots from a direct response to a presell mode to soften up the folks for his telemarketing campaigns. TV became a key to his success and profits, although it did diddly-squat all by its lonesome.

Between us, I don't think that TV alone can do the trick for many products and services. But as a medium for mass marketing, demonstrating, or *preselling*, it is a champion. Telemarketing, although fairly successful before the use of TV, is now wildly successful for this guerrilla company. And the secret to the success of both is their *combination*.

It has long been known that direct mail response rates jump from 6 percent to 22 percent when combined with telemarketing. And it has been proven many times that direct mail response rates can double, triple, and even quadruple, when combined with print advertising.

These days a *combination of marketing weapons* is necessary to succeed in a fiercely competitive marketplace. This seems to work best not with a combination of mass media such as radio or TV spots, newspaper or magazine ads, but with a combination of one or more of the above *mass marketing media* and a *direct marketing medium* such as telemarketing, direct mail, or personal sales calls.

Guerrillas call this the two-step. The first step softens up the market, asking very little, often offering something for free such as a brochure or a consultation. Step two goes smack dab for the order, and it's easier to get because the prospect has been conditioned. Can you actually condition a human being to make a purchase? Of course you can. That's what marketing combinations are all about.

Conditioning the prospect

If you've been relying exclusively on step one or step two of the two-step, this guerrilla recommends that *you utilize both*. The combination is what will bring in the business. That means you're going to have to create the combinations that work best for your business. Learn about them from industry publications, from media-buying services, and from experi-

Keep it a secret   menting. Once you learn them, don't spread the word. You don't want any competitor to know that his direct mail hasn't got a chance of success unless he attends a certain trade show and establishes a presence in a trade magazine.

This is valuable information to a guerrilla. In time, you'll find several combinations that add luster to your bottom line.

Let's face it. A single billboard isn't going to make a company profitable all by itself. Yet a retailer in the Midwest uses a downtown billboard one month per summer to support his summer sale and reports that this is his biggest month of the year. The one year he skipped the billboard was the one year he had poor sales that month.

The billboard reminded people close to his store that he had a summer sale going on, rekindled unconscious memories of his newspaper ads, TV spots, and direct mailing that month. By itself, it would have been a waste of money. In combination with other weapons, it was a money machine. Why doesn't he use it any other month of the year? It is reserved by other companies that most likely have also discovered the magic of a winning combination.

I have seen many winning marketing combinations — a computer education firm that ran several *newspaper ads* for a *free seminar* at which many new customers signed up; a marketing firm that *mails a brochure* with a questionnaire on personality types, then invites prospects to *fax the answers to the questionnaire and receive by return fax* a description of their personality; and a bookstore that combines *free author lectures* with *in-store promotions* and *signs* for those authors' books. Sometimes over 100 people attend a free author lecture. These three marketing combinations prove that one plus one equals far more than two.

Two jobs at once   When combining media, you've got to do two jobs at the same time. The first is to make each marketing effort *self-contained*, just in case the reader or viewer hasn't seen your other marketing and needs the whole story. The second is to make each marketing effort work *with the other* for readers or viewers who *have* seen your other marketing.

For these prospects, *be consistent*. Build upon the companion marketing by repeating its main points, maintaining its same style. If your efforts remind people that they've heard your message before, you've succeeded.

Marketing combinations are like one-two punches that do the job far better than a single blow. For many companies the combination consists of five punches rather than just two.

Few weapons can do the whole marketing task alone. For the most firepower, the best use of resources, and surest path to profits, follow this golden rule and combine your artillery.

Guerrilla Gimmicks

Guerrilla Marketing's Golden Rule #36:
Despite the solidity of the guerrilla's commitment to a plan,
sometimes a guerrilla's gotta have a gimmick.

THE SPIRIT OF guerrilla marketing is characterized by a serious dedication to a previously agreed upon marketing strategy. The spirit also embraces the element of amazement — marketing in ways that will actually stop people in their tracks.

You've got to do what nobody else is doing and get the undivided attention of your prime prospects. Although you would think that guerrilla marketing is bedrock common sense, now's the time to expand that thinking to include the notion that occasions arise when guerrilla marketing can mean off-the-wall tactics that win attention, hurt no one (except the competition), and earn plentiful profits.

Off-the-wall tactics

Just as you may have figured, guerrilla gimmicks are inexpensive and effective. To get your creative juices flowing, which is my way of inviting you to dream up some gimmicks of your own, feast your mind on these successful tactics:

- A very personalized mailing included a piece that looked like a full-page newspaper ad *with a Post-It stuck on it.* Handwritten on it was "Daniel, try it. This works! — N."
- A U.S. software company did a *mailing from England* with two British stamps. The first line of the letter was "While traveling in the United Kingdom on business . . ."
- A computer retailer gives presentations to schools and small businesses while peering through *a huge floppy disk.* The marketing nets him customers and great PR in the media.

- A heating firm did a mailing. At the top was typed "February 25, 1991, 9:31 A.M., *outside temperature 12 degrees below zero.*"
- A pub borrowed 25 crabs from a pet store and publicized a *crab race.* Crabs raced on a table in the pub. Nearly 400 people showed up. The winner was Crab-o'-War. And the pub owner.
- A baker makes his deliveries in a van painted by an art student to look like a *giant loaf of bread.* An Italian restaurant has a van that looks just like a *hero sandwich.*
- A retailer bought several inexpensive used cars, washed them, and parked them in his lot because empty lots are uninviting, but *lots with customers make stores enticing.*
- A jeweler displayed a diamond ring *spilling from a full box of Cracker Jack.* Another displayed jewelry on Cabbage Patch Kids dolls. A third showed solid-gold animals with animal crackers.
- A store owner calls consistent attention to his windows by placing "a mystery initial" in the front window each week. If *your last initial matches it,* you get substantial discounts.
- Some retailers make their slow days *senior citizen days.* Simply post circulars in senior citizen centers.
- *Four-leaf clovers* increase the value of a mailing and make a lovely free gift. The cost is 36 cents each, wrapped in cellophane. Contact The Clover Specialty Company at 913-321-2420.
- A restaurant owner got permission from quality motels that had no restaurants to place a three-by-five-inch index card in each room inviting guests to *bring in their motel receipt for a free cocktail.*
- Green and blue stamps aren't as popular as they used to be, but you can *give stamps to customers who purchase,* along with a stamp book. When it's filled, they get a great gift. Even better, keep a purchase card on file and offer half off on a pair of shoes for every ten pair they buy.
- A company mailed its *Christmas cards in May,* just ahead of a postal rate increase. Each card showed Ben Franklin,

Christmas in May?

our first postmaster, and the quote "A penny saved is a penny earned." Result: national PR and a high response.

- A new store donated $400 to the *local high school drill team* if they'd rehearse in front of the store during rush hour or on Saturdays. Again, grand response and free PR.
- If you ever have a contest where people must come to your premises to enter, place the entry box *in the rear of your place* so entrants have to walk past all of your offerings.
- *Hold your own olympics* by sponsoring sports competitions for underprivileged children. Give trophies and tell the press. Some businesses have many entrants in their 10K runs. Imprinted T-shirts publicize these events and your business. A client of mine had his entire company, a media-buying service, enter a 10K race. As a practicing guerrilla, he had the name of his firm on the front of each runner's T-shirt; the back was imprinted with "How am I running? Call 312-527-3747."

Picture-perfect marketing

- A remodeling business hired a student photographer to take photos of 500 homes, then *mailed the photos mounted on postcards to the home owners*. It got incredible results for a $250 total outlay.
- A consultant sent a *crisp, new dollar bill* with his mailing as a sample of what his services could bring to his prospects. Profits from one customer covered the mailing.
- A company hired a highly paid PR professional to get the company's president on a major talk show, in this case, NBC's *Today* show. The PR pro charged $10,000 for his time and effort. The company gained over $2 million in revenues directly attributable to a 50-second interview on the show.
- A dying disco directed all its marketing to senior citizens. It was the first time the club had aimed at such a target, the first time the seniors had been targeted. Naturally, the golden-agers loved the disco sound.
- A mild-mannered businessman, introverted by nature, converted himself into a superhero for his TV spots. The commercials attracted a lot of attention, and because the

superhero was clearly connected with his product benefits, the marketing gimmick worked. Such gimmicks
can also backfire, so watch out. Being amazing is risky   **Risky business**
business.

- Does your community need any signs? If so, offer to provide them, with the name and address of your business
printed tastefully on the reverse side. You may get not
only new business, but free publicity for your efforts.

It's not necessary to engage in these types of tactics on a regular
basis, but it certainly adds zest to your marketing and calls
attention to your business. These gimmicks, defined as "in-
genious or novel devices . . . used to promote sales," can easily
be incorporated into your marketing plan and calendar. They
can also be analyzed and evaluated for their effectiveness.

Often a gimmick turns out to be the most profitable marketing technique used in a year. Don't bank on gimmicks, but
follow this golden rule to engage in marketing that amazes
your public and impresses your CPA.

Not for Do-It-Yourselfers

Guerrilla Marketing's Golden Rule #37:
Let a pro produce your marketing materials, because even a hint of amateurishness can lose sales for you.

THERE ARE FEW THINGS more frustrating than producing your own printed, video, or audio brochure, getting it into the hands of prospects, and receiving zero or negative response. Yet this mistake happens time and time again.

There are few things more gratifying than investing heavily in the production of marketing materials, then enjoying a return in profits that is far higher than your production investment, along with a raftload of new customers. This also is a commonplace occurrence — among guerrillas.

Let a pro do it   The more you know about marketing, the more you'll realize the good sense it makes to let a professional production house handle it for you: the strategy, goal, selling concept, writing, graphics, models, lighting, props, shooting, sound, music, announcing, special effects, editing, and that's just for television. Print marketing requires knowledge and judgment in just as many areas. The producing of great marketing is far, far more laden with detail than can be covered in a single rule, even a golden one. It is not a do-it-yourself project.

If you've got the spirit of a guerrilla, *you have the guts and intelligence to delegate the production of your marketing.* I am one of Earth's firmest believers that you should never do what you can delegate. This comes from seeing all too many instances of marketing campaigns that disintegrated because the owner insisted on producing his own marketing.

The owner of a computer software company received straight A's in English while in college. His girlfriend was a talented artist whose paintings were exhibited and sold. Couldn't they create their own brochure and ads? Couldn't they write their own letters? Couldn't they develop their own telemarketing campaign? The answer came with the demise of their company. They used hardly any of their marketing investment in producing their materials. They wrote and designed all their own, thinking they would save money. But his prowess in English 201 and her skill at creating gorgeous oil paintings didn't generate a healthy profit for their software.

The rule of thumb is to invest 10 percent of your marketing budget in producing marketing materials. Frequently, that means 15 percent the first year and 5 percent the second. However much you do invest must be protected by someone who has knowledge in eight critical areas:

Investing in production

1. The first is the knowledge that a clear, focused *strategy* comes before anything else. Without it, you are creating and producing in a vacuum. Talent in any of the marketing disciplines — electronic, print, direct mail — is too precious to waste by being aimed at the wrong target.

2. The second is the *primary offer and benefit* you are communicating with your printed or produced piece of marketing. If you are armed with a guerrilla marketing strategy, they'll be aimed at the right target. You have the knowledge right now that the right offer and benefit will make or break your marketing piece. But do you have the knowledge to generate the right offer and identify the right benefit? Professionals usually do.

3. The third is the skill required to *write* absolutely everything in your marketing — scripts, ads, brochures, letters — the gamut. Your consistently high grades in English probably weren't based on your ability to motivate people to part with their money. Writing marketing materials has very little to do with writing compositions, essays, articles, or books. Getting a person to cry with a poem is very different from getting a person to pull out her Visa card with a direct mail letter.

4. *Graphics* aren't really number four as much as they are an integral part of number three. The great marketing minds

aren't as much writers and art directors as they are *marketing materials makers*. They think not in words or pictures, but in concepts that express their own words and pictures. The more you separate the writing from the graphics, the weaker your marketing materials will be. Still, your expert must know his way around design, eye flow, typography, color, scale, and perspective.

5. The art of *electronic sound production* requires knowledge of how best to put across your offer by blending sounds — voices, music, and sound effects — and if necessary, synchronizing them with the visual action that will accompany them. You audition five female announcers. Which is best to deliver your script to thousands of listeners? Your expert had better know.

6. *Video production* is an art and science so complex that sound production is but a teeny-weeny part of it. Here you **All the art forms** combine all the art forms — acting, set design, music, writing, choreography, graphics, special effects — solely for the purpose of marketing a product or service. You've got to be part entrepreneur, copywriter, designer, computer expert, and editing genius. The technology changes at hyperspeed. It's difficult enough for even the pros to keep up. Can you be confident that you can do it with excellence? Go bungee-cord jumping from the top of Mount Everest if you must take risks, but don't produce your own TV commercials or marketing videos. Avoid the temptation to do it yourself because there are too many places to go wrong: pace, emotions, intellect, words, pictures, music, and sounds. All must be right to advance your sale.

7. To do *print production* you've got to know the intricacies of paste-up and making your materials camera-ready. You've got to know about copying techniques, printing techniques, methods of economizing, photography, illustrations, colors, paper stock, and the differences in production requirements for the various media. Advertising agencies have huge departments to do only print production. Do you really think you can do it right all by yourself?

8. The final area of expertise you require is *judgment.* Sorry to inform you that this is not something you delegate. **Something not** You've got to be the person to know whether the people han- **to delegate** dling the other seven areas have their heads on straight. Maybe your designated guerrilla can help you judge the early stages of your marketing materials — the layouts, the rough drafts, the scripts, the thumbnail sketches. Even when you're working with pros, it is you who gets the credit or blame when your marketing succeeds or fails — because you make the final decision about what is good and what is bad. To help you, remember the yardstick of profits. If what you see will motivate people to buy what you are selling, it is good. Otherwise it is bad. This golden rule — and the professionals it recommends — will guide you to the maximum good and the minimum bad.

Part Four

Golden Rules to Guide Your Actions

Spying

Guerrilla Marketing's Golden Rule #38:

The more you spy on your competitors, your industry, and yourself, the more opportunities you'll find to improve.

ONE OF THE MOST important tools for a guerrilla is a clear picture of reality. Business owners who understand this do what they have to do to learn the truth rather than any façades or party lines.

These entrepreneurs realize the enormous significance of doing *absolutely everything* better than their competitors. But how can you be sure you're doing that?

Easy. By spying. On competitive companies. On your own company. On your own industry. And more important, on yourself.

When you, or a friend (because your voice may be too recognizable), call a competitive company, you place an order and make a request. Then you see how your order and request are processed.

Go undercover

Next, place an order and make a request at your own company. See how your order and request are processed. See if the competitor is doing *anything* better or faster or smarter than you. If so, make changes.

Have a friend visit your premises to transact some sort of business. Have the friend do the same with your competitors. Learn if they're doing things that you should be doing. Your company continues to improve as you continue to learn of ways that others do things better than you.

Visiting premises is a valuable spying technique for other reasons, too. I know a man who visited over 100 stores throughout the nation, stores competitive to his, before opening his place. He did it with the hope of getting at least one

100 spying missions

good idea per store. He ended up with one good idea per ten stores, which showed him that the level of competition was not very high, but still netted him ten dandy ideas. They are ten of the reasons he is extremely successful.

Five of the ideas that I recall for this entrepreneur's women's clothing business were

1. Forming a club and giving membership cards
2. Holding private evening sales for customers and friends
3. Mailing newsletters with discount coupons in them
4. Rewarding employees instantly and in cash for extra quality on the job
5. Never opening in a location that would not allow him to use a neon sign

There were other ideas, as there will be for you when you develop an appetite for spying. Go out into your community, out on the road, into America's major markets. Visit successful operations (get your clues from industry publications and the Yellow Pages). That's how ideas are found.

The guerrilla I describe found his ideas partly through his own imagination and partly by being an avid spy. Even his drive home takes him past two of his own and one of his biggest competitor's outlets. If you rely only on your imagination, as many business owners do, you're depriving yourself of an incredibly rich source of good ideas.

Spying is both inexpensive and informative. As with many other marketing tactics, it should be practiced regularly, at least twice a year — and more if you're serious about being a guerrilla.

Your ally, the truth   The truth will always be a valuable ally to you. One way to get to the truth often involves rolling up your sleeves and getting your hands dirty. Truth-finding is a dirty job. If you're too high-profile to be a James Bond, enlist the aid of a friend — not a business associate — to spy for you.

Let's examine five ways that you can do more than snoop.

1. *Ordering*: Buy something from yourself. Buy something from your major competitors. Do it by phone or mail or in

person, whichever will give you the best reading of the difference between you and the competition. You may have to employ phone, mail, and in-person shopping. Keep an eagle eye for the smoothness or rough edges of *the entire process*. There will be differences in many areas, more than you think. Do what you must to surpass all competitors in all areas. A good place to start: note when they do their first follow-up marketing to you. Bet you can do it faster. If not, you're up against another guerrilla.

2. *Visiting*: Unless nobody ever visits your place of business, take the time for yourself or your appointed spy to visit your place as a customer might, along with the places of your top competitors. Note all the differences, especially the little things that win or lose prospects. Don't misread the power of tiny details.

3. *Phoning*: Call for information. Request a brochure or price list, or simply ask questions. Call your competitors, too. Concentrate on the personality and attitude of the person who answers the phone. Notice the latent company strengths and weaknesses in these phone contacts. I hope the strengths are yours. If not, spying shows you exactly where you must make improvements.

4. *Comparing*: Now that you're gleaning the lessons of undercover work, compare, through a prospect's eyes, your own and your competitors' *service, pricing, packaging, people, selection, follow-up, signs, business practices, quality, marketing, delivery*, and *post-sale attitude*. As a guerrilla, you are competing in many arenas. To succeed as a guerrilla, you must be the superior entry in all of those arenas. Only spying will give you honest feedback on how you're doing. The opposite of a spy is an ostrich.

Guerrillas aren't ostriches

5. *Owning*: It will always help you to own the product or use the service of your competitors, because owning is the essence of down-and-dirty spying and enables you to spot your own deficiencies as well as your own advantages. In addition, if your competitors are public companies, buy one share of stock in each of them. Owning their stock will give you access to their annual reports, shareholder meetings, and their com-

munications with shareholders. You can learn quite a bit from this information. Don't forget, however, that your prime purpose is to learn how to improve your own operation.

Spying is perhaps the best way to learn about where your company fits in the spectrum of the competition and how it is perceived by customers and prospects. Prepare, in your training to become a guerrilla, to be confronted with some awful truths about your company when you compare it with others. There is a very small chance that you are doing *everything* better than *everybody*. Yet that's your mission.

Competition is always out there offering lessons in survival, pointing the way to excellence. Most small, medium, and large companies do not realize the treasury of brilliant marketing concepts available as everyday business in their industry — *to be spotted only if they spy.*

Once you have accomplished your spying, you must react to what you have learned. Share your findings with the rest of your company. Let them know what they're doing that's better than the competition; let them know what they're doing that's worse than the competition.

No sabotage, please

Invite them to spy along with you. Just be sure they know that the purpose of spying is to legally make yours a better company. No peeking behind closed doors is necessary. And sabotage is not part of spying. The basic requirements are a keen sense of observation and an open mind.

The businessperson of the future understands that improvement must be constant and doesn't occur in a vacuum. Following this golden rule of self-scrutiny and the scrutiny of others shows you when and where improvement is mandatory.

Achieving Credibility

Guerrilla Marketing's Golden Rule #39:
Create a path of least resistance to the sale by paving the path with credibility.

FACE UP TO IT: prospects aren't going to buy what you sell if you don't have credibility. They're not going to call your number, mail your coupon, or come into your store. They won't see your sales rep, talk to you on the phone, or accept your free offer.

Time is fleeting. Your prospects can't afford to waste it or their money with people who haven't earned their confidence. Small wonder that *confidence* has been proven the single most important reason that prospects become customers. You probably knew that all along.

In order to earn that confidence — no easy task as you've most likely learned — you've got to use specific guerrilla marketing weapons and use them properly. You've got to get down to the business of achieving and deserving credibility.

All your marketing materials, whatever their stated or pictured message, also carry a "meta-message" — an unstated, yet powerful communication with prospects.

Your meta-message

The meta-message of a superbly written direct mail letter for Deuce Cleaners on very inexpensive stationery is going to be quite different from the meta-message of the same letter for Ace Cleaners on costly stationery that looks and feels exquisite. The paper carries a strong meta-message. The meta-message will also be in the type in its dark, crisp, sharp readability. The signature will look real. Maybe it will be in blue ink.

Not surprisingly, the Deuce Cleaners letter, even though it's worded exactly like the Ace Cleaners letter, will not draw as healthy a response because of its weak meta-message. *The meta-message fails to inspire confidence.* If you don't earn confidence, you don't make the sale. Ace Cleaners knew that, so it invested in materials to convey a potent meta-message. It earned confidence with good paper and type.

Entire marketing plans fall by the wayside because inattention to seemingly unimportant details undermines the prospect's confidence, even if that confidence was earned elsewhere.

An amateurish logo makes you seem like an amateur. Any hint of amateurism in your marketing indicates to your prospect the potential for amateurism elsewhere in your company — throughout your company.

Does this mean that cheap stationery, fuzzy type, and a black signature destroy credibility? No. But shabbiness in these areas doesn't *contribute* to your credibility either. And the lack of it can — for not much extra money.

Everything you do   *Absolutely everything you do in the universe called marketing influences your credibility.* The influence will be positive or negative, depending upon your taste, intelligence, sensitivity, and awareness of this power.

Be aware of it the moment you start operating your business. Begin the quest for credibility with weapons such as the name of your company, your logo, theme line, location, stationery, business card, package, brochure, business forms, interior decor, even the attire worn by you and your people. The building you're in? An important part of your credibility — if customers come to you — but hardly relevant if they don't. Unless your building is the White House.

When amassing these weapons, keep in mind their omnipresent meta-message. It must convey your honest identity. All weapons should put forth the same meta-message — a positive message that fits comfortably with everything else in your marketing and with the reality of your offerings. You don't need a Cadillac identity to succeed with a bait shop. The truth is, a sign with the wrong meta-message can hurt your business. If you sell discount merchandise but have a slick sign, you might frighten away bargain hunters who know a pricey emporium when they see one.

Once your business is off and running, you can gain credibility with the guerrilla marketing weapons of quality — not generally recognized as a weapon, but without it you're defenseless — proper telephone demeanor, neatness in your interior and exterior, service, regular customer follow-up, and your willingness to invest time, energy, and imagination in your marketing.

Credibility weapons

If you do well in these areas, you'll activate a host of other guerrilla marketing weapons. Most will add substantial credibility to your operation. These weapons include involving yourself in the community, joining clubs and associations, soliciting testimonials from customers, and staying in touch with a growing list of satisfied customers who, most likely, will tell others about you — especially if you give them a gentle guerrilla nudge with your marketing. Word-of-mouth is priceless in the battle for credibility.

You can take shortcuts to credibility by penning a column for a publication, writing a book, conducting workshops, giving seminars, and making speeches. These help establish your expertise, your authority, your credibility.

Gain major-league credibility with a professional public relations effort, saying the right things to the right people at the right time. Once you've done that, get reprints of the newspaper or magazine articles, frame them, make them part of your brochure, and mail copies to customers and prospects. To succeed at public relations, you're going to need solid news and close publicity contacts with the media. If you don't have them, you can gain access to them via PR pros. Professional public relations people know influential editors on a first-name basis. That's almost as powerful as a golden rule.

The enormous credibility that comes with publicity stories or appearances is not inexpensive, to be sure. But if you want credibility in a hurry, PR can obtain it for you. Naturally, your trade show displays can enhance your credibility. So can any free demonstrations, free consultations, or free samples you offer. Do glitz and glamour enhance your credibility? They sure do.

Get it in a hurry

A guerrilla
shortcut

A guerrilla shortcut to credibility is a full-page ad in a re-gional edition of a respected national magazine. The ad won't net you much credibility, but the reprints you display, mail, incorporate into other marketing, and proudly disseminate *will*.

All the credibility that millions of readers attach to the magazine they suddenly attach to you. This is not to say that you wake up one day and you're *Time* magazine, but that your signs, laminated artwork, enormous posters, and future bro-chures can say ". . . as advertised in *Time* magazine." And that's just one of a bevy of prestigious magazines that offer you credibility in the form of regional editions.

To learn more about regional editions, call your local me-dia-buying service or check the consumer magazine edition of *Standard Rate and Data Service* at a good library. It's a guer-rilla secret hidden within a guerrilla golden rule.

Restraint

Guerrilla Marketing's Golden Rule #40:

Don't fix it unless you're absolutely positive it's broken.

THE HEAD OF one of the world's most famous advertising agencies, David Ogilvy, was once quoted as saying, and I paraphrase, "I see my job as being divided into two parts: one, creating great advertising, and two, getting my clients to keep their damned hands off of it."

When the Philip Morris Company launched Marlboro, it spent several years as the thirty-first largest-selling brand in the nation. And it had a feminine identity. When the idea of a cowboy and a fictional land called Marlboro Country was presented to the Philip Morris honchos, they said, "Looks good to us, let's run with it."

A full year later, after TV, magazine, newspaper, and billboard ads featured a rugged cowboy lighting up in Marlboro Country, the brand was still the thirty-first largest selling. And it still had a feminine identity. This was not good, because back then males were doing most of the smoking.

But the Philip Morris execs were committed to the campaign, as all guerrillas are, and they allowed it to run unchanged. Today, with the same cowboy figure and the same western countryside in its ads, Marlboro is the largest-selling cigarette in the land by a long shot, and it has a definite masculine identity, yet many females smoke it as well.

The unchanged cowboy

The quote by David Ogilvy shows the need to use restraint when it comes to changing your marketing. The success of Marlboro drives home the same point.

It is difficult to exercise restraint in changing your marketing when coworkers, friends, and family are counseling you to change it because they're bored with it. It's tough to use restraint in making major marketing overhauls when competitors are rocking your boat, when *Fortune* 500 companies are beckoning your prospects with enticing special effects, and when you see the marketing of others and figure that if they do it, you should, too.

But you've got to use restraint because, as a guerrilla, you know that the thing that makes marketing work more than any other element is noticeable commitment. And because you weren't born last week, you know by now that noticeable commitment implies restraint.

Companies that have learned the value of keeping their damned hands off the marketing include Green Giant, which continues to "ho-ho" after fifty years; Maytag, whose repairman has been lonely for forty years; Starkist, whose thirty-something Charlie the Tuna still isn't good enough for them; Allstate, which continues after forty years to remind us of its "good hands"; Hallmark, which just before each Valentine's Day, Mother's Day, and Christmas reminds us to "send the very best"; and United Airlines, which has been telling us to fly its "friendly skies" since 1963.

And I haven't even mentioned Ronald McDonald, the Campbell's Kids and their "Mmm-mmm good," quaint old Orville Redenbacher, Prudential's Rock of Gibraltar, Budweiser's Clydesdales, and a host of other advertising critters whose masters exerted the superhuman effort to succeed at restraint.

I also haven't singled out for proficiency at restraint several local and specialty companies such as Smith & Hawken, Mrs. Fields, Ben & Jerry's, Land's End, Book Passage, Smartfood Popcorn, and Bruce Bolind of Boulder, Colorado. They may be small and regional, unable to prove their restraint with millions, but they're guerrillas and they're successful.

Any guerrillas in your hometown?

Some of the current hotshot corporations are enjoying healthy profits with aggressive marketing, but I see a lot of them crashing and burning and I don't want you to pin your ideals on a flash in the economic pan. I point you in the direction of marketing that has strengthened the companies it has served over a long period of time. Guerrillas are in it for the long run, not the quick buck.

A guerrilla marketer is aggressive, explores new avenues of marketing, and constantly experiments and tests, but is guided by an omnipresent restraint.

It is easier to be aggressive, to explore, and to experiment than to use restraint. But once you've committed to a marketing plan and a marketing campaign, victory will come only if you enlist restraint as an ally.

The timeworn conservative adage "If it ain't broke, don't fix it" should apply to every case of marketing. But restraint appears to be in short supply. Business owners feel this uncontrollable urge to do *something* with their marketing. The something to do is to *leave it alone*.

All your brainpower and creativity is supposed to be used at the very start when you are developing your marketing strategy, not after your marketing campaign is under way. Sure, you'll have ideas for using new marketing weapons. A guerrilla is always on the lookout for such opportunities. Use them, and use them with vigor. But don't do it at the expense of your past marketing. Don't undo what you've already done. Add to it, but don't change it.

If you feel you must take action, actively maintain your current marketing efforts. As a guerrilla, you're marketing with several weapons, operating on several fronts. Do everything you can to make certain you are achieving excellence with all your weapons. Eliminate the duds and maximize the ones that demonstrate the most firepower.

The idea is to fine-tune your marketing, but don't tune it out completely. Work within the same format, the same identity. If your competitors are all doing something wonderful and you're not doing it, by all means do it. But unless you are thoroughly convinced by events of the day that changes should be made — make no changes. Your mandate as a guerrilla marketer is to have a hands-on attitude about your marketing at the outset and a hands-off attitude once it has been launched. **Hands on, then hands off**

It is not easy to leave your marketing alone. And you shouldn't. You should constantly perfect and expand it. Notice, that does not suggest that you change it.

Until your marketing is at least one year old, you probably

can't tell whether it's broken or working. And if you don't exercise restraint during this time and you start making fixes, you may be breaking something that's about to work smoothly and take off to surpass your most optimistic projections.

When people study marketing, they study *how to do it*. Right here and right now, you are learning *how to leave it alone*. To many a businessperson, leaving it alone is harder than getting it right. So they tinker and they alter and they fail. To avert such a failure doesn't take genius, nor does it take an infusion of cash. All it takes is restraint.

No tinkering allowed

The whole idea is to *get it right in the first place*. If bright people agree upon a strategy, and marketing materials fulfilling this strategy are tested successfully, that means you got it right.

If you got it right, get it going. Some companies think they're supposed to constantly improve it when the truth is they are usually innocently sabotaging it with their meddling. Guerrillas, when struck with this urge, go out and jog, eat an apple, do fifty sit-ups, or ride their bikes. They do everything they can to avoid improving their marketing, knowing time will do the job for them. The golden rule of restraint guides them.

Second in Line

Guerrilla Marketing's Golden Rule #41:
It is wise to aim to be first in line when your prospect buys,
but it is more profitable to be second in line.

IF YOUR CASH NEEDS are so acute that you require the quick
fix of a cash infusion *now,* that cash shortage is not the only
problem in your company.

Find the others or perish. Guerrilla marketing can't save a
malfunctioning business. The very nature of the guerrilla
marketing attack — *sustained offense* — is going to cause an **Sustained offense**
expansion of everything, including problems. Is it too much
for me to ask you to make your company perfect? That's what
you'll have to be to earn your position as second in line in the
hearts, minds, and purchase plans of your prospects.

Often your empty pockets, inability to secure credit, desperate situation, or lack of vision forces you to direct all your
weaponry toward making sales right this moment, trying like
crazy to be the first in line for the prospect's business. And
money. This certainly seems logical.

Such a shortage of vision has doomed many business owners as they started and operated their short-lived businesses.
Although they were probably planning on staying in business
for the long haul, it didn't work out that way because their
marketing was oriented to being first in line.

Guerrillas know they must look beyond the first place in
line. The second place in line has much to be said for it.
Reason? *Those who are first in line tend to screw up first, too.*

Remember, 80 percent of the business lost in America is **Where do**
lost due to apathy after the sale. Businesses that are first in line **ignored**
tend to **customers go?**

- Ignore their customers
- Render less-than-caring service
- Fall short of quality expectations
- Be late with deliveries
- Raise prices a mite too high
- Keep callers on hold too long
- Fail to show up on time for an appointment
- Be outgunned in the area of convenience
- Do something to lose the confidence of their customers

Where do you think those mistreated customers go? *They go to businesses that were second in line in their mind.*

It is possible to render superb service, to not mess up in any way, to aim to be first in line, and to stay there from Day One. Wal-Mart comes to mind. That's about all. The bankruptcy courts have dockets full of companies that tried this but fell down somewhere along the way. We know where. In the area of customer follow-up. In the details so small someone stopped paying attention.

It's rare to be first in line. So how does a firm get to be second in line? The answer lies a few pages back: with a *sustained marketing offensive.* Put your company second in line with the guerrilla marketing weapons that can be utilized in a

Nonstop marketing nonstop manner. There are 100 weapons, but many need not be repeated. After all, how many times do you have to write a marketing plan or come up with a logo?

Still, there are high-powered weapons that you should employ consistently in order to become second in line and in order to maintain your eventual place as first in line. The most effective of these weapons are

- Your *community involvement,* either with your local or industry community
- Your *referral program,* the systematized method you have of seeking new customers from current customers
- Your *sales training,* so that high energy is maintained and the best sales points are imparted and repeated

- Your *advertising*, to remind prospects you're alive, why they should contact you, and to motivate that contact
- Your *networking*, so that you can determine the problems of your prospects and get to know them better
- Your *phone demeanor*, whether outbound or inbound, to prove that you're an easy company to do business with
- Your constant offers of *free consultations*, *samples*, *demonstrations*, *seminars*, *gifts*, *speakers*, and the like
- Your *fusion marketing* arrangements, which prove that other companies accept you so maybe you're worth a try
- Your *service* even before the sale in the form of educating and helping your prospects
- Your *newsletter*, which tells more than it sells and gives you constant awareness, your ticket to the line
- Your *spying*, which helps you spot your weaknesses and others' strengths, so that you may have no weak spots ever
- Your *brand name awareness*, which makes time your ally, consistency your policy, and assures your place in the line
- Your *designated guerrilla*, who will ride herd over the multitude of marketing weapons you employ, especially these
- Your sense of *competitiveness*, which stimulates you to use a wide assortment of weapons on a constant basis
- Your *follow-up*, not only with customers, but also with prospects as you inch forward to the front of the line

Consistent use of these tactics and attitudes will put you just where you want to be — *for now* — second in line. As a guerrilla, you will be only a temporary fixture in that esteemed place. And you'll be second in many lines. Your commitment to marketing will propel you into first in many of those lines. That's a comfy position, looked upon by guerrillas as their permanent home. **Second is okay for now**

Because guerrillas realize that *marketing is a process and not an event*, they will earn their second place in line, then first in line. They will maintain first place as their home because they understand the need for continuous market- **A process, not an event** ing. The world changes. Marketing changes. The competitive situation changes.

Other companies, some of them guerrillas, will move up to second in line behind you. But guerrillas hang onto their customers because they've practiced and lived the principles behind this golden rule.

Proving You Care

Guerrilla Marketing's Golden Rule #42:
More companies will fail than succeed in business, and the
ones that succeed will be the ones that prove they care.

YOU CAN SAY all the fancy phrases, spice up your offer with
the proper words, and pepper your mission statement with
statements of customer love, but your dedication to service
does not come to life until you prove to your customers —
and your prospects — that you really do care about them.

Customer *care* is different than customer *attention*. Many
companies lavish attention upon their customers, but few ex-
cel at caring. Guerrillas know of more than a few ways of
starring at customer service.

Care is more
than attention

You can use some or all of these 20 ways guerrillas prove to
their customers and prospects that they sincerely care:

1. Have a *written document* outlining the principles of
   your customer service. This should come from the
   president.
2. Establish *support systems* that give clear instructions for
   gaining and maintaining service superiority.
3. Develop a *precise measurement* of superb customer service, and reward employees who practice it consistently.
4. Be certain that your passion for customer service runs
   rampant *throughout the company,* not just at the top.
5. Do all you must to instill in employees who meet your
   customers a truly *deep appreciation of the value* of
   service.
6. Be *genuinely committed* to providing more customer
   service excellence than anyone else in your industry.

7. Be sure that everyone who deals with customers *pays very close attention* to the customer. Customers should feel this.

8. Ask questions of the customer, then *listen carefully to the answers*. Ask customers to expand upon their answers.

9. *Stay in touch* with your customers: by letter, postcard, newsletter, telephone, trade shows, and questionnaires.

10. Nurture a *human bond* as well as a business bond with your customers. Do favors for them. Educate them. Give gifts. Play favorites. Take them to the ballgame or the opera. Your customers deserve to be treated this special way. If you won't do it, someone else will.

Play favorites

11. Recognize that customers have *needs and expectations*. You've got to meet the first and exceed the second.

12. Understand why huge corporations such as 3M define service quality as *"conformance to customer requirements."*

13. *Keep alert for trends*, then react to them. McDonald's operates under the axiom "We lead the industry by following our customers."

14. Share information with *people on the front line*. Disney workers meet regularly to talk about improving service.

15. Because customers are humans, *observe birthdays and anniversaries*. Constant communication should be your goal.

16. *Consider holding mixers* so that customers can get to know your people better and vice versa. Bonds form.

17. *Invest in phone equipment* that makes your business sound friendly, easy to do business with, and professional.

18. Design your physical layout for efficiency, clarity of signage, lighting, handicap accessibility, and simplicity.

What customers value most

19. Act on the knowledge that what customers value most are attention, dependability, promptness, and competence.

20. When it comes to customer service, Nordstrom department stores may be doing the best job in America, though Disney is giving them a run for their money.

The Nordstrom service manual is eloquent in its simplicity: "Use your good judgment in all situations. There will be no additional rules."

Proving you care is paying attention to the details. There are a slew of them. One large national airline figures that it exists as "one moment of truth" at a time. A "moment of truth" is any contact any customer has with any person in the organization. This airline estimates *it has 50,000 moments of truth* **Moments of truth** *per day*. Its goal is having each of these moments managed to come out in the customer's favor. If they can see it, walk on it, hold it, hear it, step on it, smell it, step over it, touch it, use it, even taste it, if they can feel it or sense it, it is a moment of truth — a tiny detail that added to the thousands of other details proves their enormous power to influence purchases.

Think in terms of educating your customers. Quad/Graphics, a Wisconsin printer, keeps customers abreast of technology by sponsoring "camps" at which customers learn how to get the best printing values. H & R Block finds both tax preparers and tax clients by offering classes to the general public. Home Depot home improvement centers and Williams Sonoma kitchen stores prove they care by showing customers how to use the things that they sell.

When things go wrong, prove you care by seeing to it that the customer comes out on top. The best return policy: "If you bought it and you don't like it, we'll take it back and give you a complete refund. Period." By the way, research shows that about 30 percent of all business problems are caused by the customer. That leaves you with 70 percent of the baggage. You prove you care by making things right 100 percent of the time, no matter who is at fault.

It's easy to appreciate a *grateful* customer, but smart companies prove their mettle in the way they treat *complaining* customers. They solve the problem first and deal with the red tape later. They also know that complaining customers can be assets to guerrilla companies. Guerrillas pay close attention to complaints.

A complaining customer has decided there is something in

the relationship worth saving, or the customer wouldn't complain. Studies have proven that for every complaint you hear, there are 24 others that you don't hear. Be alert for consistent complaint patterns. Make the necessary repairs.

Say you're sorry   Be sure to apologize when something goes wrong. That alone may be enough to convince many customers to give you another chance. Apologies don't cost you anything. Neither do written apologies that follow the verbal ones.

Do all that you can to eliminate complaints completely. Of course, that's probably impossible, but you'll be proving that you care. Make it easy for customers to express their feelings about your service by means of postage-paid questionnaire cards, suggestion boxes, and letters to key customers asking for suggestions. This also proves you care, indicates trouble spots, and guides you through the fine points of this golden rule.

Givers vs. Takers

Guerrilla Marketing's Golden Rule #43:
Companies that think of what they can give to people fare better than those that think of what they can take.

SOME COMPANIES give gifts to customers. Some publish free newsletters. Others give parties or free seminars. There are a few companies that give all these things and more. But some companies never give anything away. All they do is take.

As a customer, would you be more attracted to a giver company or a taker? As a company marketing honcho, would you describe your own company as a giver or a taker? If you're a practicing guerrilla, your firm loves to give. And you know that customers love to receive.

You hear about an apartment building with a 100 percent occupancy. That's not too unusual until you learn that the building is in an area where similar apartment buildings have only 70 percent occupancy. All the apartment buildings in this section of a major city are in the same neighborhood, charge the same rents, have the same square footage, and offer basically the same amenities. Then you dig a little deeper and learn that the fully occupied building offers *free auto grooming* with each rental.

Free auto grooming

Free auto grooming? What the devil is that? It's a guerrilla marketing weapon that pays enormous dividends. It's also a service greatly appreciated by tenants.

Someone is hired to wash the tenants' cars weekly. Regardless of what you pay the person, it's a tiny sum compared with what 30 percent vacancies would cost. The zero-vacancy building is *giving something*, not just collecting rents. You'd think that a small thing like a free car wash wouldn't be a determining factor in where a person would live. But it can be, especially in times of recession. A car wash seems like a little thing in the overall scheme of life, but little things can carry enough weight to knock a prospect off the fence and into your place of business.

It boils down to this: some companies are giver companies that relish giving things away to entice prospects and breed customer loyalty; other companies are taker companies that offer nothing for which they don't charge.

Do you think the prospect knows the difference? You can bet your bank balance on it. Although they might patronize a taker company, people would rather give their business to a giver company, all things being equal.

What kinds of things do giver companies give besides free auto grooming? Wal-Mart, America's largest retailer, arranges for a person to greet you warmly when you enter the premises and ask you what help they may render. Because the greeter receives nothing from you except, hopefully, a smile, this is a giver tactic.

Giver companies are playing show-and-sell, a game prospects appreciate, and they've seen a distinct relationship between how much they show and how much they sell. Does **Giving means** that mean that giving means getting? It does indeed.

getting   These days, there are more opportunities than ever to become a giver company. In case you haven't noticed, we're smack dab in the beginning of the age of the electronic brochure. Smart companies are giving away free videos, free audiotapes. Sure, these tapes are doing a selling job if they're properly created, but they're also doing a good job at prospect **Favorable** relations and favorable association. People will feel good about **association** your company if you create a favorable feeling with a free gift, a thank-you note, a lecture for which you charge nothing but give plenty.

Crackerjack didn't get to be a classic American snack by flavor alone. That little free gift in the box, sometimes worth less than a tenth of a cent, attracted more business than all the caramel popcorn and peanuts that surrounded it.

Giver companies curry favor (and profits) by giving bribes, free samples, demonstrations, free consultations, posters, booklets, even helpful catalogues and other publications. These companies might pen a column for a publication read by prospects. They don't charge the paper for the column. All they ask is a byline listing their company and perhaps its phone number.

They may offer speakers at no cost to community organi- **Give till it helps** zations. The speakers give information of value to the audience, selling nothing and asking nothing for their time and data. It's hardly surprising that the people in the audience tend to patronize the companies these speakers represent. After all, they've proved their expertise.

The idea, as practiced by the landlord with the free auto grooming, is to *give people more than they expect.* This is at the core of a guerrilla's attitude about business.

It is not difficult to do when you consider that much of what you can give comes under the title of service. That means many freebies are free of cost to you. You needn't invest a fortune in advertising specialties to become a giver company.

Think of the services or products or gifts or data that you can give away for free. Once you act upon what you've generated in your brain, yours can become a giver company, too. And prospects will magically transform into paying customers. Only it won't be magic. It will be generosity.

Giver companies seem to be — and often really are — more customer-oriented than taker companies. As a result, they attract more business, gain more repeat sales, earn more referrals, and pocket more profits, too.

A guerrilla puts customer service on a pedestal, then proves **Something** it by giving away items or services of value, not simply free **of value** junk. As a giver company, your company comes across as generous. Its identity is one of low rather than high pressure, because everyone knows that high-pressure firms want to take rather than give. Giver companies create an unconscious sense of obligation to buy. They generate goodwill, and they stand apart from companies that give zilch and take all they can.

Think of your customers and the types of things you can give them. Perhaps it is information. Maybe it's inexpensive electronic gizmos, often available for under $2. But if you're going to be a giver, you've got to be sure you're giving *something of value to your customers and prospects.*

The mathematics of guerrilla marketing is fascinating: the more you give, the more you earn; the less you give, the less you earn. Only a person who knows this golden rule realizes why.

Networking, Guerrilla Style

Guerrilla Marketing's Golden Rule #44:
To network properly, ask questions, listen to answers, and focus on the problems of the people with whom you network.

THE GUERRILLA KNOWS that the purpose of networking is to learn of people's problems so that the guerrilla can provide the correct solutions. The guerrilla sees networking as socializing with a business purpose.

Networking with the idea of selling yourself is the wrong mindset. Don't waste your energy talking. Use it to listen instead. Give other people a chance to talk. If you do your networking with the right people, almost all of those people will be prospects. One of the yardsticks by which you can measure your networking is the *percentage of prospects that become clients*. The higher that number, the better your networking.

Measuring networking

Another yardstick is the *amount of information gathered*. The more you learned, the better you networked. One more measurement: *generosity*. The more you gave, the better you networked. Give something such as important information, concisely presented, or a lead to a prospect for your prospect. The more your tidbit of data helps the person you told it to, the better you did your networking. These are among the potpourri of opportunities for the guerrilla networker.

In the 1960s, networking was associated with progressive, even radical, organizations that shared information on themes such as peace, the energy crisis, and the environment. In the 1980s, the word *networking* became part of our mainstream vocabulary, used by everyone from budding entrepreneurs to the giant AT&T, which suggested that businesspeople do more of it — on the telephone.

By 1989, *Webster's Dictionary* defined networking as "the exchange of information or services among individuals, groups, or institutions." It did not identify it as the superpower marketing tool it can be for a guerrilla.

A pure form of marketing

Networking is an honest and natural way to establish trust and nourish relationships. It is personal marketing in a pure form. Many of the guerrilla marketing weapons are involved: your attire, your personality, your enthusiasm, your credibility, your neatness, your smile.

Your job is simple: ask questions. Home in on the problems faced by the person's company. Probe by asking more questions. Tell your reasons if you're asked about your curiosity: your company markets solutions to many problems; perhaps you can help this person who is becoming both a business contact and a friend.

Your networking strategy

To do the best job of networking, create a written strategy — that's right, a networking strategy. It requires only three pieces of information and keeps you on target in selecting networking sessions and getting the most from them.

A networking strategy states first the purpose of your networking, possibly to learn of problems your company can solve. Then it lists the item of value you will be giving away, maybe a piece of information of value to the people at the gathering. Finally, your strategy outlines the groups with whom you will network, so that you know which invitations to seek and which to turn down. It is better to enter a networking situation with this data than without it. Otherwise you have a good chance of getting distracted by the sounds of other networkers blowing their own horns.

Armed with marketing materials in the form of business cards or minibrochures — now you know why so many guerrillas have business cards that double as minibrochures — you seek out conferences and conventions your prospects are likely to attend.

Don't waste your time joining peer networks unless you want to establish alliances. Go where the prospects are. Community events are often a rich source of contacts. But you may have a company that could gain zero new business from such events. Network with discrimination.

Contacts are always good to have, and the more the better. But contacts are a by-product of networking. *Problems* are the pot of gold at the end of the rainbow. Allowing prospects to talk with you about them will enable you to show your understanding and to offer helpful advice. It will serve as an ideal springboard for your future direct mail and telemarketing to these prospects. You'll be able to refer back to your conversation about the problem. You'll be able to set the stage for your solution.

Your prospect will remember you because you're the one who asked all those questions and listened so attentively. You even took notes! And you came up with a couple of bright suggestions.

Guerrillas take notes

Networking is also an ideal forum for bartering. As long as they are not your peers and competitors, some people in the group will be more than willing to trade their products or services for yours. Sometimes this is the right way to make purchases. I've done it several times and have no regrets. To the contrary, I have a solar heating system, giant-screen TV, and memories of two first-rate cruises as a result of bartering. Some of that bartering came as a result of networking — and seemingly the trade arose from nowhere. I was asking questions, that's all.

If a guerrilla wants a convenient networking situation, the guerrilla *creates* it. You need four elements to succeed:

Creating networking opportunities

1. A guest speaker with a hot topic
2. A chance for all in attendance to introduce themselves, make an announcement, and hand out a card or brochure
3. Things to eat and drink
4. A list of the right people to invite — your prospects

Give careful thought to what you'll say when you introduce yourself and make your announcement. Because you'll be doing a whole lot of listening and not much speaking, this is your big chance to say the most important thing you can during the few seconds you have.

Planning what you'll say is the only way to proceed if you're serious about succeeding in life. Winging it is wasting a precious opportunity. I've seen people blow it during these situations more than I've seen them shine.

You know that *time* is the investment you will be making when you begin to network. That means you must spend your networking time only with people who can become major customers. Don't be charmed by that person who might be dandy at the beach, but is a waste of your time at a networking function. Guerrillas keep their priorities straight. Did I say it was easy?

Establish relationships with a small number of people. You want closeness, not quantity. You can't find out a person's problems in just minutes. But if you limit your networking conversations, you can get a good start on your task of spotting problems.

There will always be more networking functions where you can meet more people. At each gathering, limit your conversational partners, but not your conversational intensity. This is easy to do with questions. Questions reveal problems, and this golden rule leads you from problems to profits.

Pioneering

If you're going to pioneer with a new product or service,
you must be prepared for walls of apathy and fear.

NO DOUBT ABOUT IT, there's a heady and exciting feeling that comes with announcing to the world a brand-spanking-new product or service — especially one with a clear and dramatic customer advantage. But for every giddy delight, there are fifteen hidden horrors. Pioneers get to do it first, but they often end up with arrows in the back of their neck. Ouch.

Guerrillas have long recognized that breaking ground often involves breaking your toe with the shovel. And this pain is not uncommon on the front lines of marketing, especially if the lines were just established.

If you are creating marketing, instead of seeking the original and conveying the idea of a breakthrough, put the odds in your favor by doing what you can to go only with the proven. Study marketing books and periodicals, especially magazines about your industry, to learn what is working for whom and how you can gain inspiration from it.

Waterbeds are now a $2 billion industry. When they first came to market, industry leaders offered partnership deals to some of the biggest names in the innerspring market. "No thanks," they were told. "We have no doubt that you'll do well, but we've been pioneers before and we don't want to be pioneers again." This attitude was due to the fact that it took twenty years for the public to switch from stuffed mattresses to innersprings. Pioneering requires patience.

It has long been said that Procter and Gamble, a Hall of Fame marketing organization, tries to be *second* on the market with its products. "Let the others make the mistakes. Let us

Hall of Fame marketing

learn from them. Then let's do it right." Sounds like a guerrilla marketing adage to me, because guerrillas can't afford to
make mistakes. They've got to get it right the first time. That's
hard for pioneers.

Contrary to public opinion, people *do not want* to be first
on their block to own anything. Instead, they'd prefer to be
seventh or eighth on their block. Twenty-sixth wouldn't be so
bad either. They've made purchase errors before and they
don't want to make them again. Waiting and seeing makes
more sense.

Experts tell us that as a rule of thumb, 2 percent of the
population instantly embraces innovations. Another 12 percent accept them after a year, and after two years 22 percent
join the band. This means that pioneers must have the fi-
nances to hold their breath for a long time. And even after
that long two years 64 percent of our citizens are still waiting
and seeing.

You can see it happening right in front of your eyes every
day with compact disc players, a big hit with a tiny group of
people in the beginning, a relatively commonplace household
item today. The same is happening with fax machines and
satellite dishes. Whether your company is developing or marketing a new product or service, in spite of the quality of your
offering, human behavior prohibits the instant gratification
you, as a normal human, crave.

If science developed an anti-aging pill and the FDA granted
instant clearance, it would be five to ten years before the majority of the population would take it. What if it has an unpleasant side effect? What if their buddies laugh at them for
trying it? What if it doesn't work? What if it's not worth the
money they pay for it? There are many mistakes to be made.

No more   People do not want to make *any* of them because in the past
mistakes   they've made most of them — or at least they know stories of
people who have.

Despite their resistance to the new, Americans accept it far
faster than Europeans. While working in England during the
late 1960s, I took part in a presentation to the marketing com-
mittee for England's most popular anti-zit ointment. We rec-

ommended TV aimed at teenagers. Their response, and this was in 1968: "While we agree that teenagers are our primary market, we are not convinced that television is here to stay." Pioneers face that attitude on a daily basis.

I suppose that it is simply human nature to resist change. This is because people have an innate fear of making a mistake. Even though people want the new offering, perhaps even need it, they will hold back until they've heard of a friend who bought and used it. Let the friend make the mistake.

Acting as a spy listening in during focus group interviews, I have all too frequently heard the reasons people have resisted new advancements: "I want to wait until they get all the bugs out." "I never buy anything the first year it comes out." "I haven't heard enough about that yet." (Even though they just read a lengthy brochure about it.) "I'll just wait. I don't know why, but I'll hold on a while before I buy it." "Maybe it causes cancer, how should I know?"

If you have the going-in knowledge that people are going to be reluctant to try your new product or service, you can capitalize on that information. Here are five things you might do to surmount the barrier faced by all pioneers:

Surmounting the barrier

1. Tell how many people have already purchased the offering and how many have already made a repeat purchase.
2. Offer more information in the form of a brochure, video, sales call, almost anything.
3. Provide a clear guarantee or warranty to assure the person that he or she will not be making a purchase error.
4. Mention the name of a person or company, known to the prospect, who has already made the purchase.
5. Help the prospect recall that at one point everything was new: television, computers, refrigerators, even cars. Tell how many people delayed their purchases because they weren't sure these breakthroughs were here to stay.

Now that I've mentioned the word *breakthrough*, I want to caution you *against* using the word. Because your product or service is new, avoid words such as *breakthrough, revolution-*

ary, and *advanced*. Let your product benefits speak for themselves and steer clear of the adjectives. Although it really may be an advancement that you offer, to the prospect it's an experiment — using the prospect's own money. The newer your offering, the closer you should stay with tried and true words. The word *proven* takes on added power if you're a pioneer.

Tried and true helps

The word *patience* takes on new meaning, too, because of the time it takes people to accept you. Be prepared to stick it out, and don't think your product or service is doomed just because people stay away in droves at the very beginning. That's the way people are. And the way pioneers react is with gentle confidence. Don't forget, your prospects are as apathetic as they are frightened by your offering. If you know that, this golden rule can help you defuse the fear and replace the apathy with enthusiasm.

Marketing in a Recession

Guerrilla Marketing's Golden Rule #46:
To succeed at marketing during an economic downturn, focus your efforts on existing customers and larger transactions.

"IN A DOG-EAT-DOG ECONOMY, the Doberman is boss," said Edward Abbey, the naturalist. In this regard, the Doberman and the guerrilla have a lot in common.

Guerrillas know that they must seek their profits from their *current customers*. They worship at the shrine of customer follow-up. They are world-class experts at getting their customers to expand the size of their purchase. Because the cost of selling to a brand-new customer is *five times higher* than selling to an existing customer, guerrilla marketers turn their gaze from strangers to friends. This reduces the cost of marketing while it reinforces the customer relationship. Guerrillas know they are marketing to some of the most cherished citizens of planet Earth — their customers.

Five times higher

When your customers are confronted with their daily blizzard of junk mail, your mailing piece won't be scrapped with the others. After all, these folks know you. They identify with you. They trust you. They know you stay in touch with them for a reason. And so they'll be delighted to purchase — or at least check out — that new product or service they didn't know you offered. They'll always be more inclined to buy from a company they've patronized before instead of experimenting with a company that has not yet won a share of their mind.

The kinds of businesses that prosper in a recession are guerrilla businesses that commenced their customer follow-up within 48 hours of the customer's first purchase with a note thanking them for their patronage. Three to five weeks later these firms sent a brief letter asking if the customer is completely satisfied and needs anything at all. Follow-up continues forever or longer and eventually produces a cornucopia of referral names.

When you follow up with this intensity, it proves you really care and you'll be there when the customer really needs you. **Admit it** In a recession the optimum opportunity is to market with a stated recognition of the recession and the way that you can help your customer shrug it off. Gear your benefits, if at all possible, to the recession. Try hard; it's worth the energy and imagination you devote.

If you haven't started a customer stroking program yet, start it tomorrow. And whatever you do, put it in writing and determine just two things: (1) who will take the responsibility for each follow-up activity, and (2) when that activity will take place.

Telephones are terrific In any recession the telephone is a remarkably effective follow-up weapon for guerrillas. You certainly don't have to use the phone to follow up all of your mailings to customers, but research proves that it *always* will boost your sales and profits. Sure, telephone follow-up is a tough task. But it works. Anyhow, no one ever said that guerrilla marketing is a piece of cake.

Important recession tactic: eliminate any perceived risk of buying from you by stressing your money-back guarantee, your liberal warranty, your deep commitment to service. Mention the names of others or the number of others who have purchased from you. Your reputation is the foundation on which your continued credibility is built, and during a recession you need all you can get. Credibility doesn't cost you anything, so lean on it as much as you can.

Guerrillas are able to think of additional products and services that can establish new sources of profits for them. In a recession or out, they are on the alert for strategic alliances — fusion marketing efforts with others. This kind of cooperative marketing makes sense at all times, but makes the most sense during a recession when companies must market aggressively while reducing their marketing investment.

Guerrilla companies cease most broadcasting and increase their narrowcasting — to customers and carefully targeted prospect lists. A recession is tough. Still, when the going gets tough, guerrillas make sizable bank deposits. Many see beauty in economic ugliness.

In a recession, when everything seems to be shrinking, think in terms of *expanding* your offerings. Do absolutely everything you can to motivate customers to expand the size of their purchase. Prove that buying right now is a sagacious move *because* of the recession. **Expand while others shrink**

If you sell high-priced items, use the recession as a selling tool. Explain to people that during a recession, it is crucial not to waste money. Therefore, they should protect their money by spending it wisely and not making a mistake. Mistakes can be financial disasters during a recession. Doesn't that make sense?

In marketing to customers and to noncustomers, show that you are fully aware of the recession and that you have priced your goods and services accordingly. Don't make the mistake of thinking that the right price for a recession is the lowest price. Price almost becomes secondary during hard times; people are searching for *value*. If you offer customers great values — in the form of more durable products, more encompassing services, or long-term economy, you'll earn higher profits than if you target your marketing solely to the skinflints.

Even though your marketing is always truthful, exert even more of an effort during a recession to make it *sound* truthful. Admit that there is a recession; admit that people must be extra careful when buying things; admit that you have taken special steps because times are tough and you know it.

The plain fact is that guerrillas have an advantage during recessionary times. They are able to work in relatively shorter time frames. Their penchant for information enables them to respond more quickly and creatively to market needs. **The guerrilla's advantage**

The guerrilla lives by different rules during a recession than during boom times. The guerrilla attacks when the enemy retreats, and the attack is concentrated where the guerrilla offers specific product or service advantages. Retreating companies leave voids in the market, ideal niches for guerrilla companies.

Guerrillas do not commit all on any front because they try to maintain resources for new options and for potential confrontations with the competition. Flexibility is an asset. Successful guerrillas try to be inconspicuous about their success, reducing the chances of copycatting and attack from competitors.

They know that many companies have scrubbed or reduced their marketing budgets to combat the recession, and that it will cost those firms three dollars for every dollar formerly spent to reach the same level of consumer recognition and share of mind they previously enjoyed. Guerrillas are aware that their prospects are more likely to recall marketing messages delivered consistently during the recession — even if they are smaller and less frequent. So they maintain the attitude of a guerrilla even when the economy is in its darkest days.

Along with their aggressive attitude is a willingness to give up something in order to preserve something else. Intelligent sacrifice is a necessity. Unless a company is governed by this golden rule during a recession, marketing may be too expensive to be effective.

Luxury Box Marketing

Guerrilla Marketing's Golden Rule #47:
*If you have an especially important client or customer,
market to that person in an especially important way.*

THE TREND IN major-league sports is to construct luxury
boxes, also known as skyboxes, where people can enjoy the
game, whether it is baseball, football, or basketball, with the
excitement of seeing it live and the luxuries of home — sofas,
easy chairs, bar, kitchen, TV, all around them.

Sometimes corporations that do a lot of entertaining purchase these luxury boxes. But they don't use them for every
game. Then do they remain empty? No, they don't, and every
guerrilla should know that they can be rented for as little as
$500 per game, and they usually accommodate about a dozen
people. At about $42 per person, that's a small price for the
experience of a lifetime. To illustrate, I'll tell you a story, a
true story:

Luxury for rent

Once upon a time, right now, to be specific, there is a guerrilla business owner who receives regular telephone calls from
his very best customers and prospects — and the calls come
directly to his home.

Sometimes those calls are to place an order for his product,
which we'll call BurgerBuns. Other times they're to arrange a
lunch, dinner, or to set the date to take in a ballgame with the
business owner.

He receives extravagant Christmas gifts from his customers,
and although he treats his best customers in the accommodat-
ing manner they deserve, they treat him even better. I need
not point out, but I will just to illuminate its unique nature,

that *this is not the normal case in business.* Not in America.
Not anywhere. But it's normal for this clear-visioned business
owner.

To help you zero in on the raw power of this golden rule,
this story incorporates a flashback of one decade. . . .

Hundreds, perhaps thousands, of packaged foods are introduced in America every year. Although many of these items
are brought out by big-name manufacturers, most end up in
oblivion. Where, oh where, is my long-lost Hawaiian Salad
Dressing?

Into this dire situation we introduce a man — a true sports
nut, but unfortunately a person who was so financially desti-
tute he was living in his car. Along with his idea. Hardly the
picture of a guerrilla, but very definitely the mindset, as you
are about to see.

Today this man runs a $10 million company, and it's grow-
ing just as fast as the owner desires — which does not always
mean speedy, as far too many forlorn entrepreneurs can assure
you as they show you their scars.

Ten million in sales is a figure that catches the attention of
a red-blooded guerrilla. How could a person with so little
achieve so much? If ever there was a loaded question, that's
it — brimming with its answer about a secret weapon.

That answer is *luxury box marketing.*

The man, who combined his interests in sports and food,
used the techniques described in *Guerrilla Financing* to raise
enough money to buy a very small company that made micro-
wavable and oven-cookable snacks. He had two target audiences. One was sports fans and kids who would eat his snacks.
The other was buyers from major supermarket chains. He figured that if he could succeed with the buyers, his products
would be so widely available that with a tiny mention in the
supermarkets' ads and the monstrous force of his secret weapon
he could succeed where others failed.

His second target, the buyers from the large supermarket
chains, was so small that you could count the people on your
fingers. That's a well-defined target.

It meant that he could exert a serious effort toward luxury box marketing. First he convinced the concession authorities in a major-league baseball park to allow him to set up test vendors of his product, just a few of them. Based upon that success, he arranged to sell his BurgerBuns at most of the concession stands. Again, a one-year test.

Next, he rented a luxury box for $500 in the stadium. At the same time, he placed an ad in the home team's program, mentioning BurgerBuns in huge letters. And he displayed the BurgerBun name inside the ballpark. He couldn't afford to place a sign on the scoreboard, but he rented sign space with good visibility.

To his luxury box, which he now rents twelve times a year, he invites the key buyers — not competitors of each other — and one new prospect per game, sometimes more than one. In addition, he invites his director of operations, his major distributors, some members of his staff, and a few current customers. Twelve people are invited to each of the games. They're picked up at their home or hotel by private limo and escorted to the luxury box, which is available for baseball, football, and sometimes basketball games in most cities featuring major-league teams.

Take them out to the ballgame

Our BurgerBun guerrilla hires a bartender who pours anything the guest may desire and a chef and waiters who serve an exceptionally delicious meal. During dinner, the business owner points out his ad in the game program and his sign facing the crowd. Since the twelve games he selects are night games with contending teams, the crowds are always impressive. Guerrillas attend to such details.

It's no coincidence that during the game an airplane circles overhead towing a banner reading "BurgerBun Welcomes SuperSave" — or whatever supermarket chain is being wooed that night. There's nothing subtle about this guy.

No coincidence

You can be sure the people in the luxury box will not soon forget the wooing. For most, this was their first experience in a luxury box and a rare ride in a limo, not to mention the private chef and free-flowing cocktails. The airplane wasn't shabby either.

I'm not sure whether it's pure cause and effect, but in the supermarkets BurgerBuns get preferential shelf space and facings. Their signs are boldly and prominently displayed. When the BurgerBun people come to supermarkets to do their demonstrations and free samplings, they are warmly welcomed, as are their products by the customers.

As you might have guessed, this business owner's expansion plan is centered strictly where major-league teams have luxury boxes. His plan is focused on the West Coast right now, and he does well enough that he need not expand anymore.

Fun and games   Many guerrillas have since discovered the luxury of skyboxes and their unique effectiveness with a small, definable market. To get to see your favorite sport played while your cheering, food, and drink are doing your marketing for you — and to do it on a regular basis — that's about as enjoyable as guerrilla marketing gets.

Luxury box marketing is only one version of what might be termed "luxury marketing." Instead of luxury boxes at sporting events, you might entertain key prospects and customers with boxes at the opera, symphony, or theater. You might invite them to luxury weekends at wilderness locations or city centers. You might have an elegant dinner at your city's best restaurant — in a private room of course. And then there are luxury cruises that last but a day, yet result in a lifetime's worth of business. I've been to several of those and I was impressed each time. Once, *I* was converted from a prospect to a paying customer.

The reason I stress luxury boxes over these other examples of luxury marketing is because the others have been around for decades and many companies have discovered them. But luxury boxes are relatively new, and the interest in spectator sports is at an all-time high. This is the type of combination a guerrilla seeks and welcomes. The guerrilla knows his prospects have been to concerts and plays before, even to elegant restaurants. But to a luxury box? Probably never.

If you practice luxury box marketing — or any kind of luxury marketing for that matter — remember that it's only part of a marketing mix. It is reserved for the most important — meaning potentially profitable — prospects and customers. And it is not appropriate in every case. Some people hate baseball. You don't ever want to alienate anyone while you are marketing with luxury. Be politically sensitive — invite the boss even if you are really seeking an order from one of her subordinates. Can luxury marketing ever be overkill? Hardly. Everybody is flattered by the attention. Luxury they enjoy. Insincerity, pressure, or even a hint of bribery is not part of this kind of marketing.

Prospects and customers who experience luxury box marketing — or luxury marketing of any sort (but not the opera in my case, please) — want to be sure they experience it again and again. That's why this golden rule is so easy to follow.

The Wisdom of Moving Slowly

Guerrilla Marketing's Golden Rule #48:
When planning and producing marketing, then evaluating
it, operating from a guerrilla calendar is indispensable.

A GUERRILLA MARKETING calendar is valuable two times
each year: number one, when planning a year's worth of marketing, week by week — so you can foresee your marketing
thrust, weapons to be used, and cost of marketing — and
number two, at the end of the year when you look back on
your cash flow figures and compare them with your marketing calendar. At that time, you'll know what bombed, so you
can eliminate those promotions, and what sizzled, so you can
double or triple those. But most important, the guerrilla marketing calendar enables you to move slowly.

Every guerrilla has learned, and probably the hard way,
that when creating marketing, there is speed, quality, and
economy. While any two may be selected, the guerrilla always opts for quality and economy. The guerrilla would never
think of reducing the quality of his marketing. The guerrilla
would want this quality at an economical price in every in-
stance. But the guerrilla is rarely in a hurry for the marketing
Scheduling materials. By scheduling the future, the calendar makes the
the future rush avoidable. So the guerrilla benefits from both quality and
economy.

Of the bevy of complaints I hear from fellow marketing producers, the most common by far is about the clients who want
their work yesterday. These clients, who comprise about 75
percent of most ad makers' client lists, are choosing speed and
quality. Economy goes by the wayside with overtime and rush

charges. In most instances, these charges are avoidable because a guerrilla marketing calendar makes the rush avoidable.

Although guerrillas are ready to make changes instantly when necessary, they do everything they can to eliminate the times that can happen. They do this by staying anywhere from *one month to three months ahead of schedule* in producing their marketing materials.

This isn't difficult when you operate with a guerrilla marketing calendar, which lets you see one year at a glance. Such calendars give you the benefit of seeing the future and stomping out potential emergencies.

No more emergencies

Although a guerrilla marketing plan is only seven sentences long, you should create each sentence with great thought, taking as much time as you need, not rushing, and recognizing that each sentence will guide your marketing efforts for years to come.

Judge the finished plan slowly as well. Regardless of how simple and straightforward it appears to you, be aware of its long-term implications for your company and sleep on it a night or two before approving it.

Sleep on it

Move slowly when you create your marketing calendar as well, although you plan only three components — marketing thrust, media to be used, and marketing cost — for each of the 52 weeks in a year. At the end of the year, when assessing the calendar in light of a fourth component — results — move slowly when making changes. You'll be getting rid of the efforts that didn't work, increasing those that did. An important job. No need to rush. Your goal is a calendar filled with proven marketing efforts.

Suppose you plan a direct mail campaign of a letter, postcard, and follow-up letter for November. Because you're making the calendar in January, you know eleven months ahead of time what you will need. Call in the copywriter and art director. Give them the assignment. You eliminate their rush charges, which are exorbitant because it's tough to create effective marketing in only one day. You also give the creative folks time to think about the assignment, draft it, improve it, polish it, and perfect it. Instead of receiving hastily conceived work that costs the moon, you get thoughtfully conceived work that is priced reasonably. But more important, you get marketing that has a better chance of working.

Give marketing a chance   Guerrillas give themselves every edge to give their marketing every conceivable chance to work. They know that tight deadlines mean shoddy work. Listen, I've been there. I've seen it happen. I've seen clients demand finished work the following day. They got the work they demanded and on time. The day after that, the person who created the marketing materials had an idea that was ten times stronger than the one submitted. Too bad. Too late.

In marketing, there are many decisions to be made, many of them subjective, and many must be made in a hurry. What color? What photo? What typeface? What model? What price? What headline? Most businesspeople do everything they can **Decision-avoiders** to avoid making decisions because a decision brings the risk of being wrong.

You want your marketing machine to be run by people who are willing to make a decision and be wrong. People with the authority to say yes or no, but without the guts to say either *create unnecessary marketing emergencies.* They hold up the works so that when the creative team is finally set loose, they're up against a backbreaking deadline.

Weed out these people. Transfer them. Send them for assertiveness training. Decisions must be made for the marketing process to proceed. Giving a creative team a tight deadline is cheating your own company. Business is tough enough without artificial bottlenecks.

David Ogilvy, advertising author and ad agency founder, said that the mark of a true professional is the willingness to make an improvement in marketing that has already been approved by the client. When you create marketing materials in a hurry, there is often no chance to make the improvement because the ad or commercial has already been produced. The need for speed robs the true professional of the opportunity to give teeth, spin, and substance to the marketing.

Each improvement you make to your store during the

month *before its grand opening* is testimony to the wisdom of moving slowly. The free PR offered by the newspaper or the coverage offered by the TV station? Don't accept it until all the details of superb service and quality have been attended to. Move slowly. The temptation is to do the opposite. But the guerrilla knows the crucial importance of a marketing calendar and the constant need to avoid emergencies. With this careful planning the calendar improves each year as success builds upon success, and all in slow motion.

Quality and economy are always important, but *profitability* and not speed is the hallmark of the guerrilla who has learned the wisdom of this golden rule.

Guerrilla Relationships

Guerrilla Marketing's Golden Rule #49:
Treat sales transactions not as single events, but as starts or continuations of close and lasting relationships.

ALL SUCCESSFUL MARKETING is based upon relationships. Sometimes they are short-lived, nonemotional, and fairly shallow relationships. When possible, guerrillas know how to turn them into lasting relationships. Each sales transaction or social interaction of any kind is an opportunity for the guerrilla to augment each relationship.

Remember, a relationship in a business sense is far more precious than a sale. Relationships lead to referral sales, repeat sales, volume sales, and dependable sales. The deeper that relationship, the greater profits the guerrilla will earn.

There is a universe of difference between a wonderful sale and a wonderful relationship. These are guerrilla words to live by.

Where relationships come from

Guerrilla relationships come from six primary groups:

1. Customers
2. Employees
3. Suppliers
4. The media
5. Businesses in your community
6. And anyone else who, with you, can reap the benefits of a mutually rewarding relationship

Besides the standard guerrilla tactics of potent follow-up marketing — letters, postcards, phone calls, free gifts, previews, discounts, and recognition by name on sight — the guerrilla deepens the relationship with a small and select group of individuals, marketing to them by educating them, actually helping them to succeed. The idea is to think tiny and keep in mind the 80–20 rule — that is, 80 percent of the profits come from 20 percent of the customers. Naturally, that means you should develop your closest relationships with the 20 percent while maintaining close relationships with the 80 percent and being careful to make them feel appreciated, too.

Think tiny

Guerrillas consider the following criteria as well when applying this guerrilla principle of investing time instead of money:

- Will the time invested in this relationship generate a healthy return on your investment?
- Who will benefit more from the relationship, you or your customer? Mutual benefit should be your aim.
- Is the relationship with one person (which is the best) or with a group of people (not a bad second best)?
- Is the customer in a position to implement the methods you'll provide for helping her succeed?
- Is there good chemistry between you? Will you enjoy the times you'll interact?

A forward-thinking company not only can define its target market, but has already begun developing a nucleus of close relationships that are mutually profitable. These relationships, although *focused on strengthening your customer's business*, can take place at restaurants and on picnics, at ballgames and on river trips, at backyard barbecues and on ski trips. Notice that golf courses and tennis courts have been left out because the guerrilla knows that the idea is to *help* and *not compete with* the customer. The idea is to leave the usual business setting and get to know more about the person as a businessperson and human being so that you can be of better service as a businessperson and as a human being.

Don't compete with customers

Everyone and his second cousin knows that people like to do business with friends. This is not to recommend that you make friendships just to gain business. Good friendships are worth more than even the best business relationships. But this is to recommend that you know as much about your customer and what would help that person as you would know about a good buddy.

Not all businesses can profit from guerrilla relationships, but if yours is one that can, look into it. You might start by looking at the books *Relationship Marketing* by Regis McKenna and *Guerrilla Selling* by Bill Gallagher, Orvel Ray Wilson, and me. Both books give valuable insights into the psychology of business relationships. The more you know about the connection between the human bond and the business bond, the better off you'll be.

The underlying concept   The underlying concept of a guerrilla relationship is *the success of the customer* — measuring success by any yardstick you pick. How do you contribute to this success? With information. With education. With attention. With tidbits of pertinent wisdom. With advance notice. With price breaks. With suggestions. If you're dealing with a business, try to think like an executive of the customer's company. Come up with good ideas — at no expense to the customer — and offer them at no cost.

Do it with newsletters, free seminars, in-store clinics, demonstrations, and samples. Talk to your customers and send customer questionnaires. Do it with your prime customers, those with whom you have the warmest guerrilla relationships. Have long talks and at different locations outside your places of business. If you can, have suggestion boxes that solicit customer suggestions. Be sure to thank *everyone* who makes a suggestion.

A key to testing your ability to maintain guerrilla relationships is to ask yourself after every customer contact, "Did I make that person feel special, unique, one-of-a-kind, an individual?" If the answer is no — you fell down on the job. Ask also, "Did we connect and do I clearly understand this person's needs?" Again, yes is the only acceptable answer.

That fine line   A guerrilla constantly walks that fine line between business and social relationships and is careful to keep a sensible balance between the two. Guerrillas do not seek to populate their social life with people with whom they can do business. But even I must confess that two of my closest friends are men who started out as my clients — another exception to the rule.

Capitalism is crass enough without having to select your friends from among your customers. Guerrilla relationships take place primarily during office hours, though exceptions can and should be made to this. As I said a moment ago, it's a fine line. Walk it so that your best customers gain valuable contributions from you as you follow this golden rule.

Eating Life

Guerrilla Marketing's Golden Rule #50:
If you don't take control of your marketing, your company's future will be in the hands of your competitors.

THERE'S AN OLD Yiddish expression, "You eat life or life eats you." This golden rule translates that wisdom into guerrilla marketing terms.

There's certainly no question that outside circumstances can dictate the success or failure of a venture. It is less well-known that you can create *inside circumstances* to compensate for the things you cannot control.

Inside circumstances

In business, you have two options. You can devote serious marketing energy, utilizing multiple weapons and solid common sense to produce results, or you can simply advertise and think that means you are marketing.

Those who practice guerrilla marketing eat life. You can be sure they are never the entrée. Marketing guerrillas cause their competitors — and their customers — to *react to them* rather than having it be the other way around. They know that if things are left to themselves, they tend to go from bad to worse. Worse yet, if it is possible for more than one thing to go wrong, as one of Murphy's laws reminds us, the thing that will go wrong is the one that will do the most damage. Guerrillas take life, circumstances, situations, misfortunes and good fortune into their own hands. They take control. They eat life.

How to do it

Their management isn't there to merely put out fires and run the show. *They manage to achieve results.* Here's how:

1. *Encourage employees to set goals.* Reward them for achieving those goals. Make sure the goals are realistic.

2. *Set goals for yourself.* Don't say, "I'll reduce costs." Say, "I'll reduce costs by 5 percent by June 30 of 1994."
3. *Be sure employees receive feedback from an expert.* The source is as important as the information.
4. *Be a coach, not a commander.* Be employee-centered more than you are productivity-centered.
5. *Give extra attention to people who perform extra well.* These are the people who will help your company shine.
6. *Cause action after meetings with a one-page statement of actions needed, who will do them, and when they'll be completed.*
7. *Reward employees with excellent attendance records.* This isn't marketing, but it cuts down on absenteeism.
8. *Cut down on the number of reports required by your firm.* Weekly reports might be replaced by biweekly reports.
9. *Give short-term assignments early on Friday afternoons.* This creates action at the time of week that needs it most.
10. *Do all hiring on the basis of attitude, not aptitude.* It's easier to teach data than to change personalities. (Hold off on doing your hiring till everyone is working so hard they'll be glad to see the new employee, regardless of where the newcomer sits.)

Guerrillas eat life by recognizing the precious and elusive nature of time. They know that time is not money; it is far more valuable. That's why when running a business, guerrillas call instead of write, ask how long it will take when asked for an appointment, have employees read trade journals and mark crucial items to save them time, streamline their business forms as much as possible, meet in other people's offices so they can leave when they feel the meeting is over and have more time control, confirm appointments by phone before leaving, and know deep in their hearts that committees take a week to do what one good person can do in an hour, especially one who eats life.

Time-savers for life-eaters

Is it difficult to spot companies that eat life? Nope, it's just the other way around. They don't do anything highly secretive in their appetite for life and their penchant for understanding the entire breadth of guerrilla marketing. These companies have a great deal in common, and it's not impossible for your **Life-eating** business to dine on life as they do.
companies

- Concentrate upon *what you do best*. The backfiring of many mega-mergers clearly attests to this rule.
- Develop *great public relations* — not merely with your public, but with your employees, vendors, and customers.
- Build *close relationships with other businesses* to maintain a constant two-way flow of valuable information.
- *Share your progress with your employees*, which is not only fair, but a wise business practice as well.
- Be sure *all levels of management are committed to the company's goals* and that they know these goals inside out.
- *Keep all your promises*, whether the promises have to do with delivery, price, selection, or whatever.
- Maintain the *highest standards of quality control*, knowing that any shoddiness will eventually be exposed.
- *Focus on customer needs* and fulfill these needs with extra-value service, giving more than expected.
- Engage in *long-term planning*, not only in marketing, but also in purchases, production, and personnel.
- Be *above the norm for investing* in marketing, as well as in research and technology within your industry.
- Insist on *reasonable returns on all your investments* all of the time; *reasonable* is the key word.
- Work productively by understanding *the crucial difference between efficiency and effectiveness*.

The essence Maybe you're wondering what the heck all this has to do with
of guerrilla marketing. The answer is that it is the very essence of guerrilla
marketing marketing. Notice that what is required to engage in these healthy practices is not necessarily a pile of money, but a pile of common sense instead. That and the ever-necessary commitment of the guerrilla.

Businesses that succeed and prosper do so by eating life. Running your business in this way requires extra energy on your part, that's for sure. But be warned that if you don't expend this energy, someone else will come along and do it instead. You'll end up as life's dessert. Don't let that happen. Eat life yourself by following this and all of guerrilla marketing's golden rules.

Epilogue

Breaking Golden Rules
*Although it's inevitable that rules — even golden rules —
are broken, it's crucial to know them inside out so you
know what you're breaking and why.*

WHEN I TOLD my wife the name of this chapter, she said,
"Yep, that's what rules are for." Not true. Not these golden
rules.

These rules have been formulated to help you improve your
business in the form of more profits, which, hopefully, you
can translate into less stress and more free time. Following
these rules helps you avoid the pitfalls many business owners
have fallen into without knowing there were rules to follow in
the first place.

As they broke the golden rules, they were unaware that they
were doing so. You don't have that convenient excuse. You
know the rules. When you break any of them, you'd better
have an extremely good reason because these rules were made
to be *followed* — up a continuously rising sales curve and into
an entrepreneurial golden nirvana.

**You have
no excuse**

If you're going to break any rules, go drive 56 miles per
hour, or tear from your mattress that tag that warns of dire
consequences if you do. But follow these golden rules, and
bear in mind that even though they are bang on target right
now, things do change — and some, but not many of these
rules will have to change, too. That's a shame really, because
business is so much easier if you have clear rules to follow.

Guerrilla marketing's golden rules offer you that clarity.
There's no shilly-shallying around the basic issues. Market like
a guerrilla and follow these rules. I never said it would be
simple. I never said it would be a joyride. I never said it would

be fast. I only said that if you run your company by these golden rules, you'll enjoy more profits and less heartache.

More profits, less heartache

Success will come easier and larger than you thought.

We both realize that there's a lot more to business than marketing. You've got to have those details down pat, or marketing, even guerrilla marketing practiced by golden rules, can't work its wonders. This book provides you with many of those details since so much of business can come under the heading of marketing. Don't let a little overlapping get in the way of your success.

Given human nature, I suppose you will be tempted, at times knowingly, to break the rules pertaining to cleverness, restraint, networking, moving slowly, humor, or originality. That's no surprise to me, because during my career I've seen these are the most commonly broken rules. But if you break them, I'll bet you don't do it more than once.

Rules you'll be tempted to break

"Ouch! That fire was hot! I sure won't put my hand in the flames anymore!" These rules prevent that painful lesson.

It's more unlikely that you'll try meddling with the rules about profits, honesty, being interesting, economizing, proving you care, or achieving credibility. You're too smart for that. If you've read this far in a book about marketing, you're not too likely to disregard rules of such obvious importance. Try to apply the same steadfastness to the golden rules that might present you with more of a challenge to follow.

Now that you understand the deep-down importance of following the rules, I invite you to go out and discover some rules of your own. Make some new rules by experimenting with your marketing. Commitment does not preclude experimentation if the experiments are conducted in test markets.

In fact, guerrilla marketing encourages experimentation and the risk of failed experiments. Don't let cold feet keep you from potentially hot ideas. If you haven't fallen on your face, you probably weren't trying hard enough, or else you were a guerrilla who knew where the obstacles were. Just realize that experimentation does not necessarily mean breaking the rules.

Okay, I've made that clear. Now let me completely change direction and invite you to *think about breaking the rules.*

Maybe you can come up with a good reason to do it. Then do it! Maybe you want to make an exception to a rule on purpose, and you've clearly thought things through, including the rule. Do it! Good luck, and I mean it.

If you break one, good luck!

My wife said that rules are made to be broken when, in fact, rules are made to be followed, but also to be questioned. Many of these rules are the answers to questions posed by guerrillas. Many are the result of following the opposite of the rule and meeting constant frustration. Many have been proven through centuries and throughout the world.

I did not invent these rules any more than Moses invented the Ten Commandments. I merely present them to you, along with my counsel to put your faith in them and trust that they will work for you as they have worked for others.

More to the point: failure to follow these rules has unraveled the companies of many other well-meaning business owners, some quite intelligent in the ways of the world, but untutored in the ways of the guerrilla.

To do yourself a favor for which you will offer yourself endless gratitude, ask yourself *why* you are breaking a rule when you do so. If you don't have a good reason, you've got a great reason to follow the rule. Be sure you *know* you are breaking a rule when you break it. At least you will be acting with purpose rather than with ignorance.

It's hard to imagine a more unfortunate waste of a company's money than to break a golden rule by accident. Do companies waste billions this way every year? Do Rice Krispies snap, crackle, and pop? At least I can take heart that *your* company won't be guilty of so wasteful an act as negligent rule-breaking.

All these golden rules combine to give you marketing insight, a good thing for a guerrilla who intends to flourish today and in the coming century. An old Chinese proverb says that if you have foresight, you're blessed, but if you have insight, you're a thousand times blessed. To those blessings, I add these golden rules.

Now You Can Continue to Be a Guerrilla with
The Guerrilla Marketing Newsletter!

THE GUERRILLA MARKETING NEWSLETTER provides you with state-of-the-moment insights to maximize the profits you will obtain through marketing. The newsletter has been created to furnish you with the cream of the new guerrilla marketing information from around the world. It is filled with practical advice, the latest research, upcoming trends, and brand-new marketing techniques — all designed to pay off on your bottom line.

Each issue of the newsletter is rich with data that can help your company. If you aren't convinced after examining your first issue for 30 days that *The Guerrilla Marketing Newsletter* will raise your profits, your subscription fee will be refunded along with $2 just for trying.

The Guerrilla Marketing Newsletter, written by Jay Conrad Levinson, is available only by subscription. The rate is $49 per year for six issues. To subscribe or to obtain information on guerrilla marketing workshops and consulting services, call toll-free 1-800-748-6444, or (415) 381-8361. Or Write: Guerrilla Marketing International, 260 Cascade Drive, P.O. Box 1336, Mill Valley, CA 94942, U.S.A.